T0109605

BREAK DOWN THE U.S. CONSTITUTION

THE INSIDE SCOOP ON
OUR FOUNDING DOCUMENT

WRITTEN BY SARA LATTA

ILLUSTRATED BY MANUEL MOLVAR

CAPSTONE PRESS
a capstone imprint

Published by Capstone Press, an imprint of Capstone
1710 Roe Crest Drive, North Mankato, Minnesota 56003
capstonepub.com

Copyright © 2025 by Capstone. All rights reserved. No part of this publication may be reproduced in whole or in part, or stored in a retrieval system, or transmitted in any form or by any means, electronic, mechanical, photocopying, recording, or otherwise, without written permission of the publisher.

Library of Congress Cataloging-in-Publication Data is available on the Library of Congress website.

ISBN: 9781669076438 (hardcover)
ISBN: 9781669076384 (paperback)
ISBN: 9781669076391 (ebook PDF)

Summary: Playful graphics and text take readers on a historical tour of the history of the U.S. Constitution and how it has changed over time.

Editorial Credits
Editor: Mandy Robbins; Designer: Heidi Thompson; Production Specialist: Tori Abraham

Any additional websites and resources referenced in this book are not maintained, authorized, or sponsored by Capstone. All product and company names are trademarks™ or registered® trademarks of their respective holders.

CONTENTS

INTRODUCTION: THE PEOPLE BEHIND THE PAPER

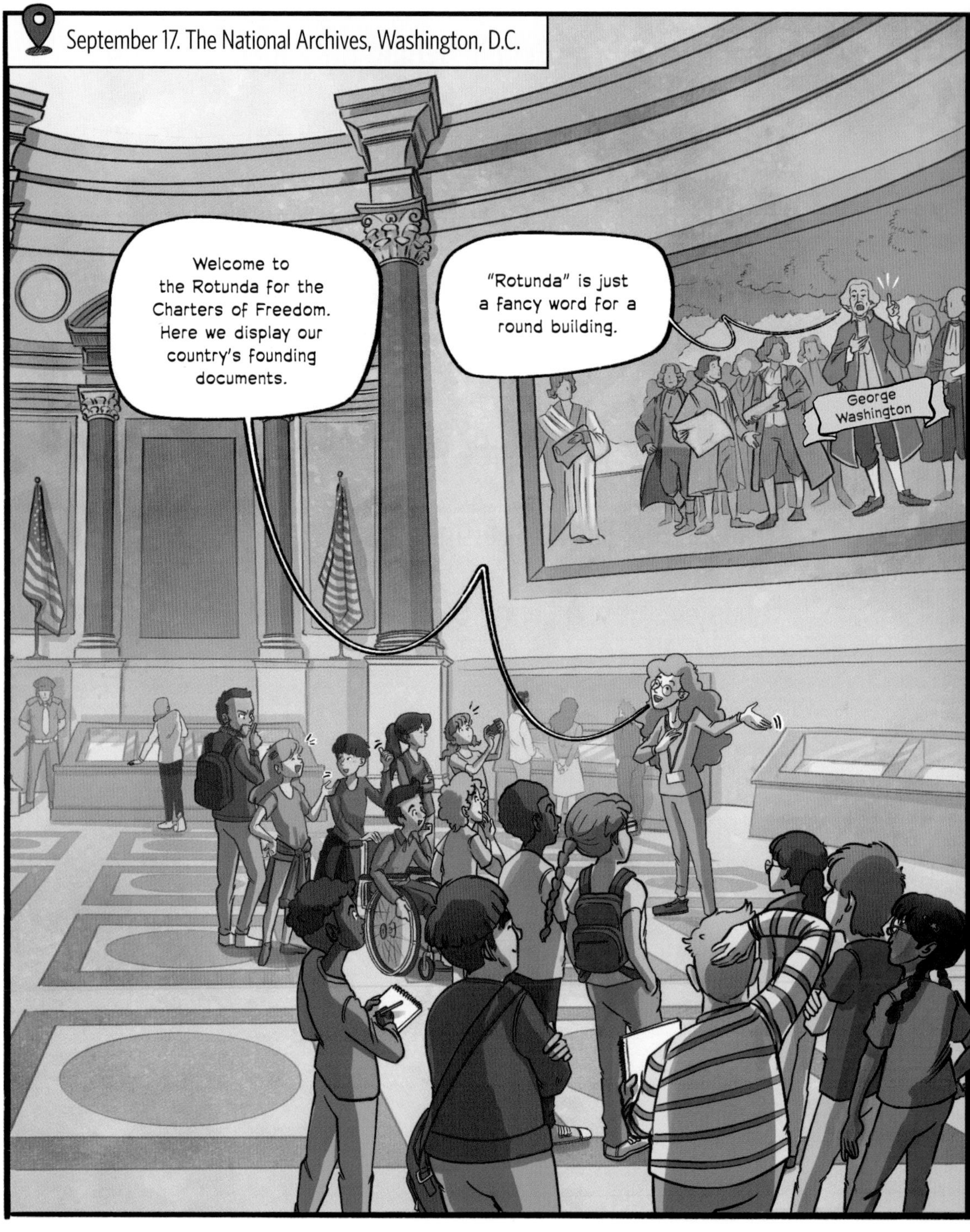
September 17. The National Archives, Washington, D.C.
Welcome to the Rotunda for the Charters of Freedom. Here we display our country's founding documents.
"Rotunda" is just a fancy word for a round building.
George Washington

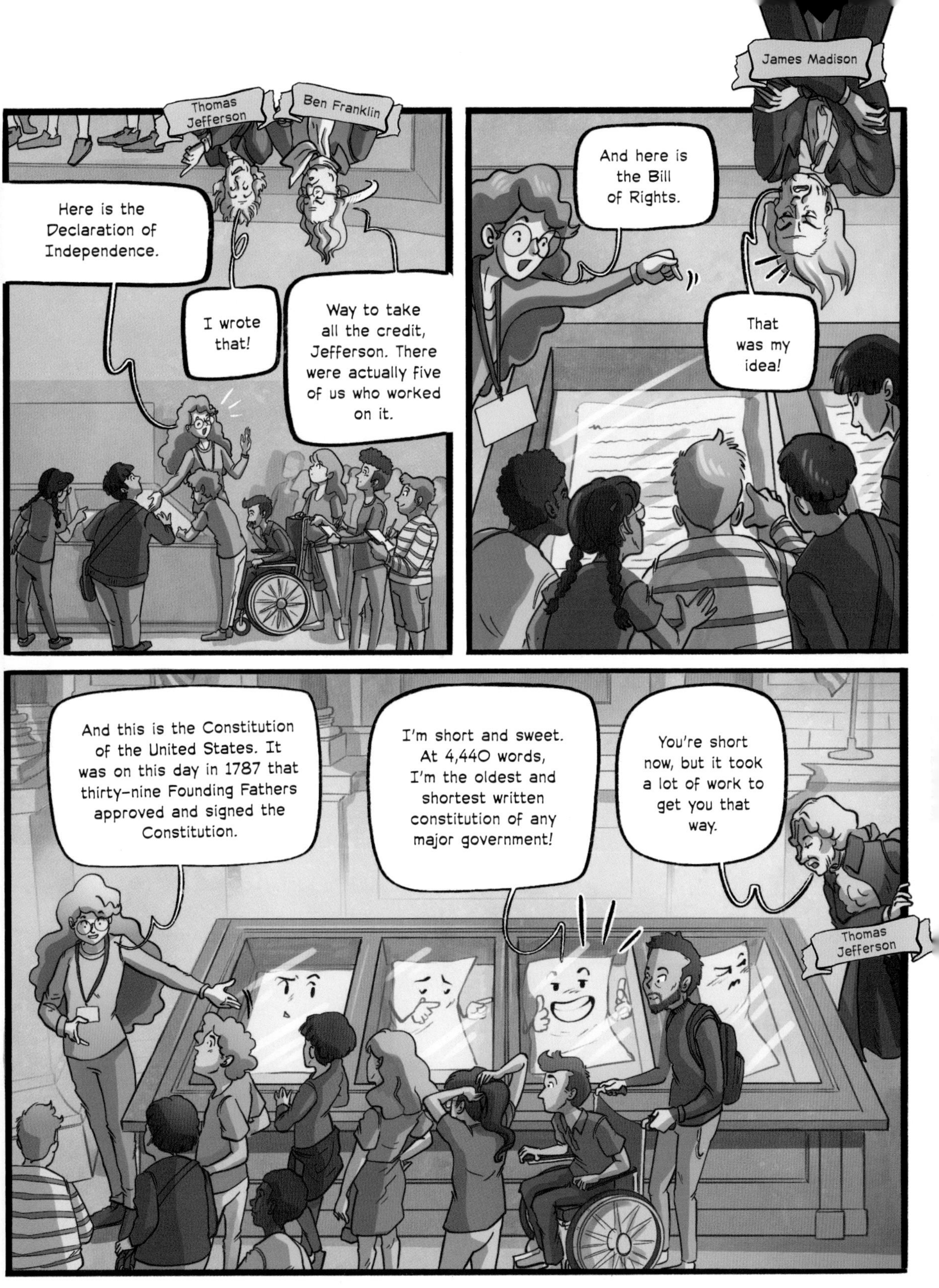
Thomas Jefferson
Ben Franklin
Here is the Declaration of Independence.
I wrote that!
Way to take all the credit, Jefferson. There were actually five of us who worked on it.
James Madison
And here is the Bill of Rights.
That was my idea!
And this is the Constitution of the United States. It was on this day in 1787 that thirty-nine Founding Fathers approved and signed the Constitution.
I'm short and sweet. At 4,440 words, I'm the oldest and shortest written constitution of any major government!
You're short now, but it took a lot of work to get you that way.
Thomas Jefferson

CHAPTER ONE: FOUNDING A NATION

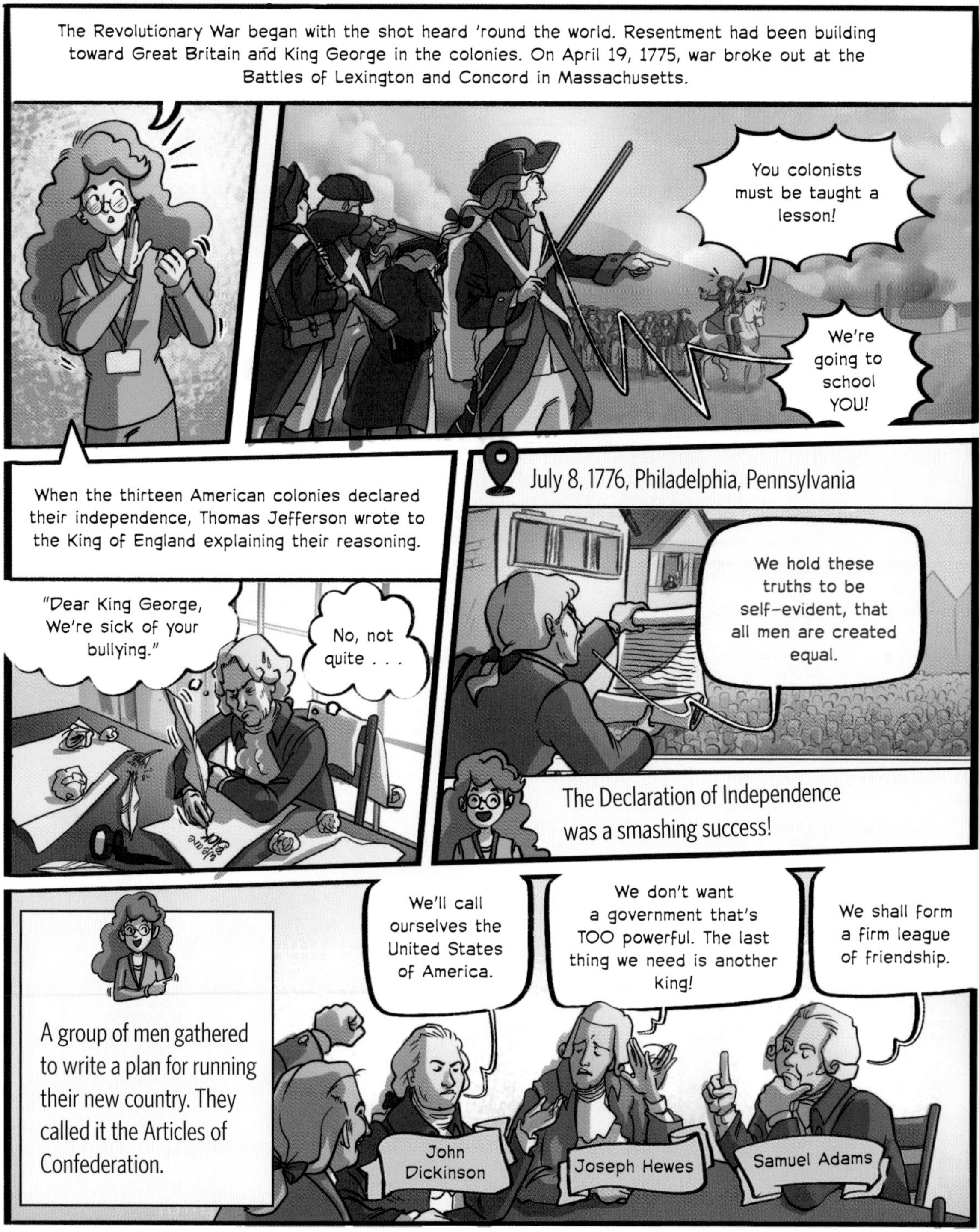

The Revolutionary War began with the shot heard 'round the world. Resentment had been building toward Great Britain and King George in the colonies. On April 19, 1775, war broke out at the Battles of Lexington and Concord in Massachusetts.
You colonists must be taught a lesson!
We're going to school YOU!
When the thirteen American colonies declared their independence, Thomas Jefferson wrote to the King of England explaining their reasoning.
"Dear King George, We're sick of your bullying."
No, not quite . . .
July 8, 1776, Philadelphia, Pennsylvania
We hold these truths to be self-evident, that all men are created equal.
The Declaration of Independence was a smashing success!
A group of men gathered to write a plan for running their new country. They called it the Articles of Confederation.
We'll call ourselves the United States of America.
We don't want a government that's TOO powerful. The last thing we need is another king!
We shall form a firm league of friendship.
John Dickinson
Joseph Hewes
Samuel Adams

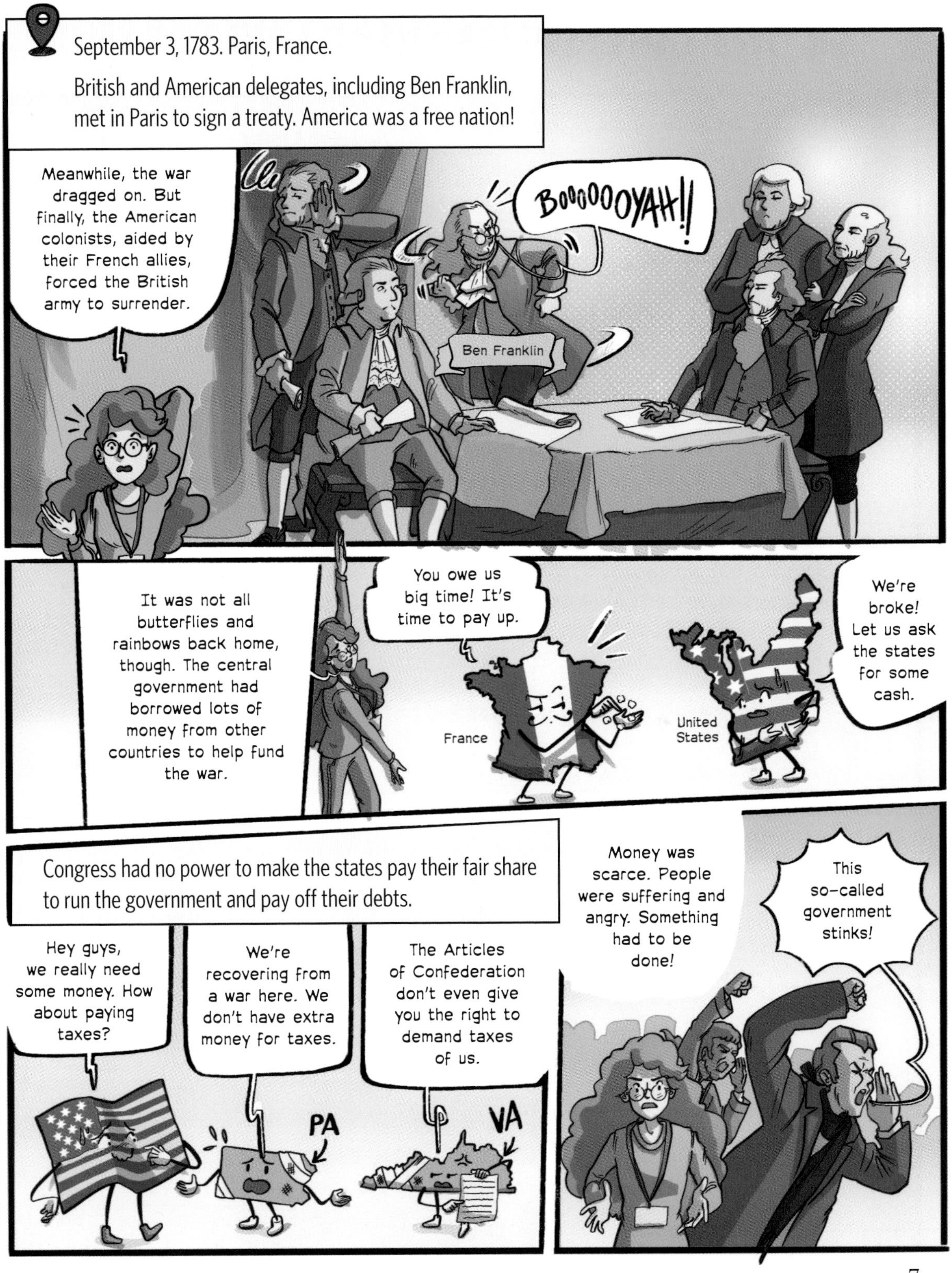
September 3, 1783. Paris, France.
British and American delegates, including Ben Franklin, met in Paris to sign a treaty. America was a free nation!
Meanwhile, the war dragged on. But finally, the American colonists, aided by their French allies, forced the British army to surrender.
BOOOOOOYAH!!
Ben Franklin
It was not all butterflies and rainbows back home, though. The central government had borrowed lots of money from other countries to help fund the war.
You owe us big time! It's time to pay up.
France
United States
We're broke! Let us ask the states for some cash.
Congress had no power to make the states pay their fair share to run the government and pay off their debts.
Hey guys, we really need some money. How about paying taxes?
We're recovering from a war here. We don't have extra money for taxes.
PA
The Articles of Confederation don't even give you the right to demand taxes of us.
VA
Money was scarce. People were suffering and angry. Something had to be done!
This so-called government stinks!

CHAPTER TWO: THE CONSTITUTIONAL CONVENTION

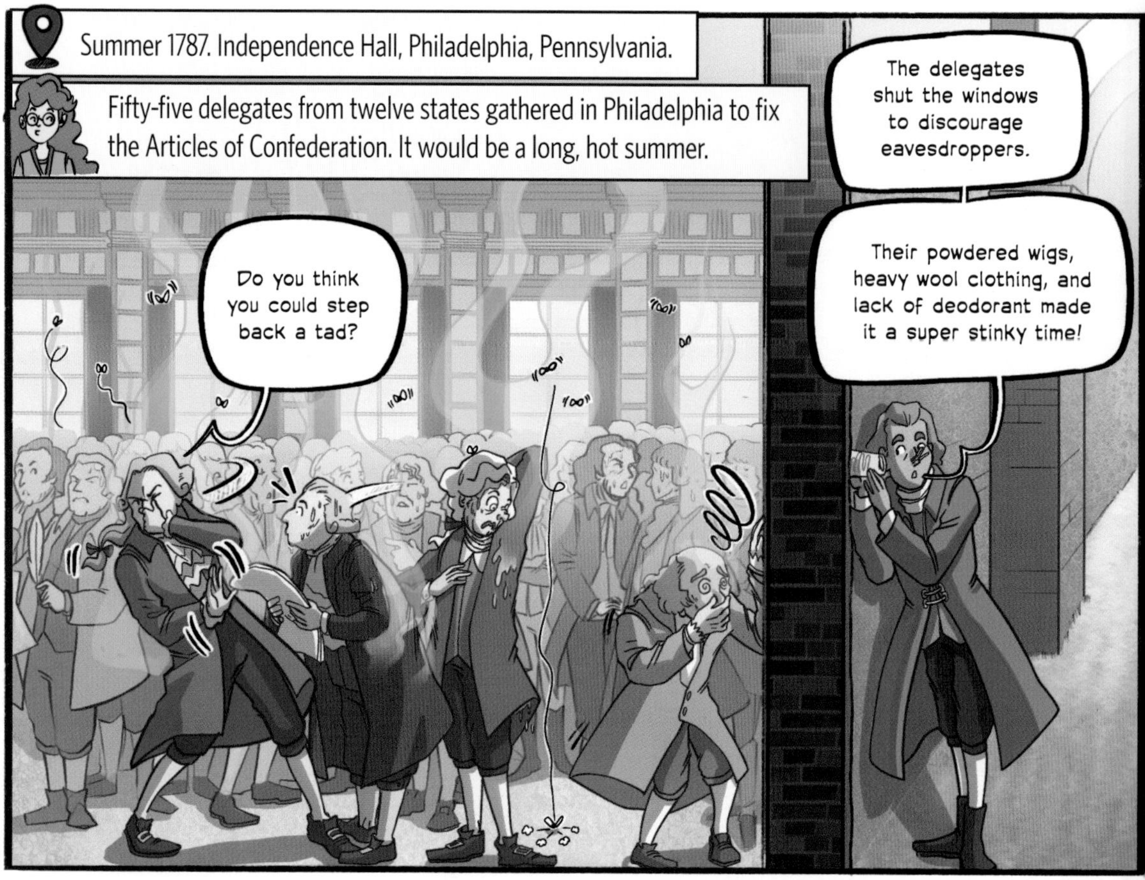
Summer 1787. Independence Hall, Philadelphia, Pennsylvania.
Fifty-five delegates from twelve states gathered in Philadelphia to fix the Articles of Confederation. It would be a long, hot summer.
Do you think you could step back a tad?
The delegates shut the windows to discourage eavesdroppers.
Their powdered wigs, heavy wool clothing, and lack of deodorant made it a super stinky time!

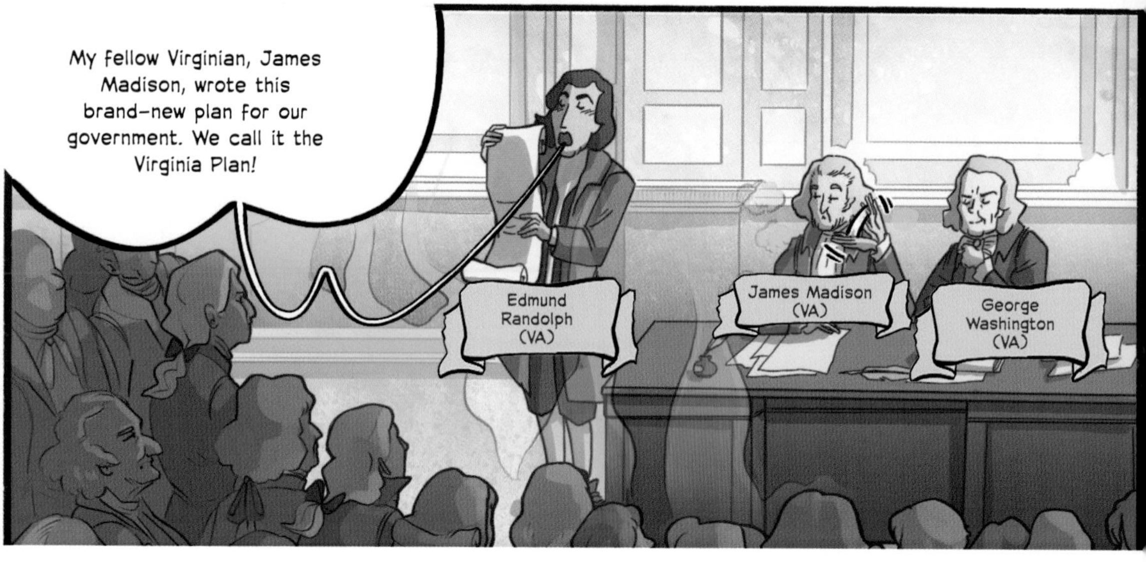
My fellow Virginian, James Madison, wrote this brand-new plan for our government. We call it the Virginia Plan!
Edmund Randolph (VA)
James Madison (VA)
George Washington (VA)

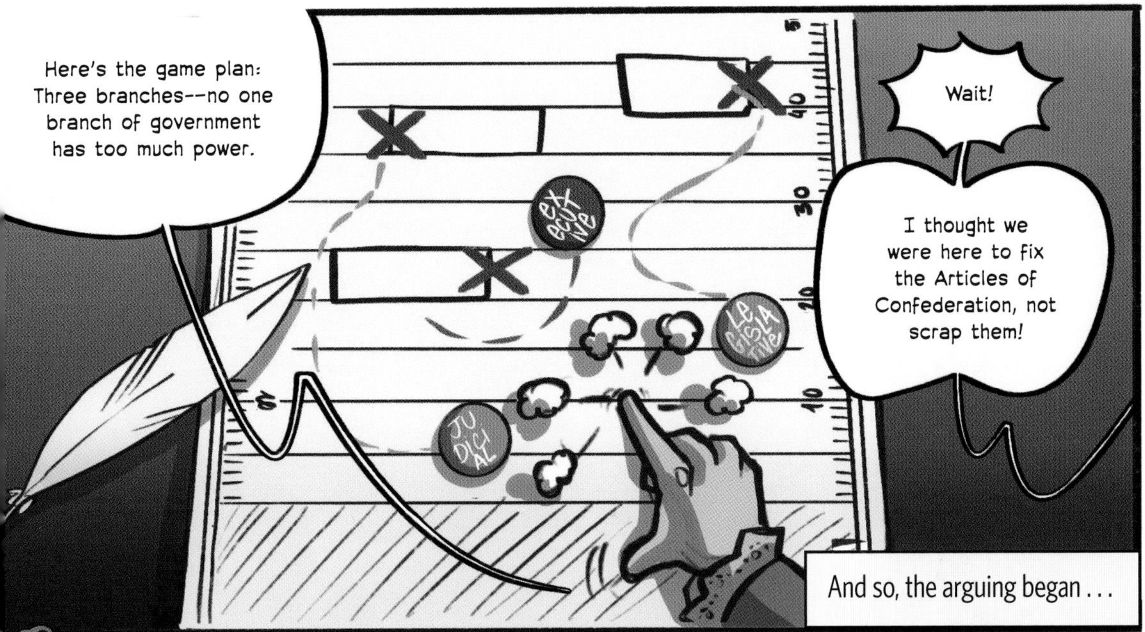
Here's the game plan: Three branches--no one branch of government has too much power.
EX ECU TIVE
LE GIS LA TIVE
JU DICI AL
Wait!
I thought we were here to fix the Articles of Confederation, not scrap them!
And so, the arguing began . . .

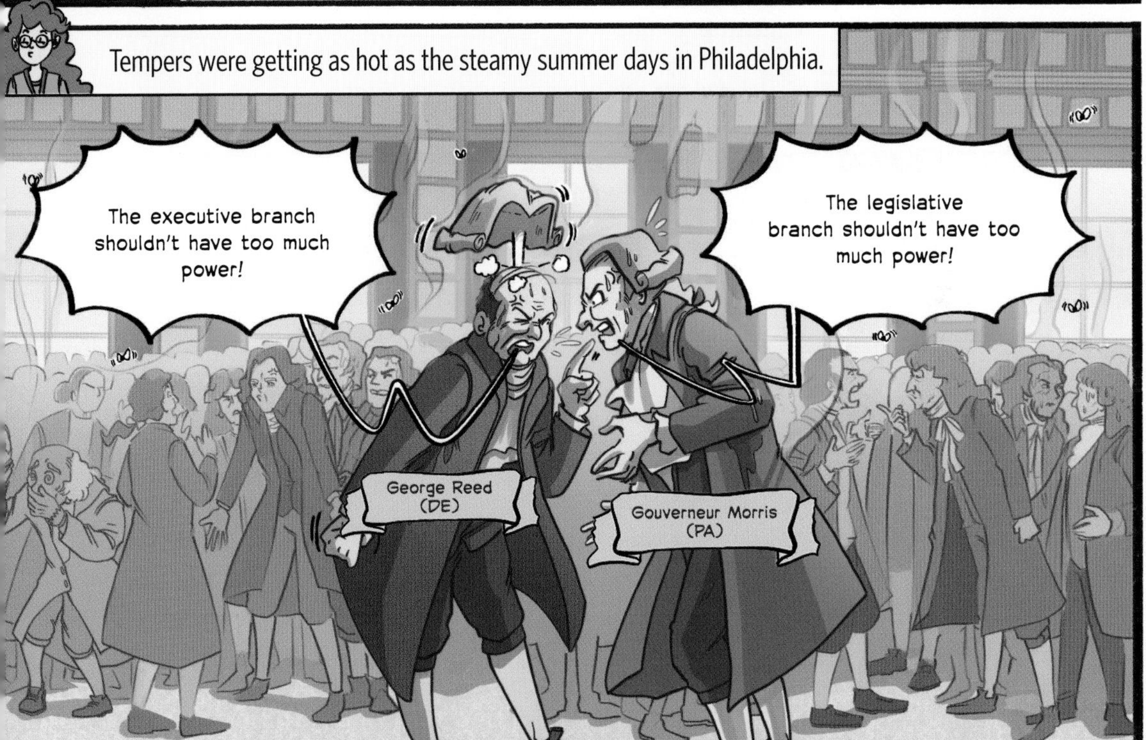
Tempers were getting as hot as the steamy summer days in Philadelphia.
The executive branch shouldn't have too much power!
The legislative branch shouldn't have too much power!
George Reed (DE)
Gouverneur Morris (PA)

THE CONNECTICUT COMPROMISE

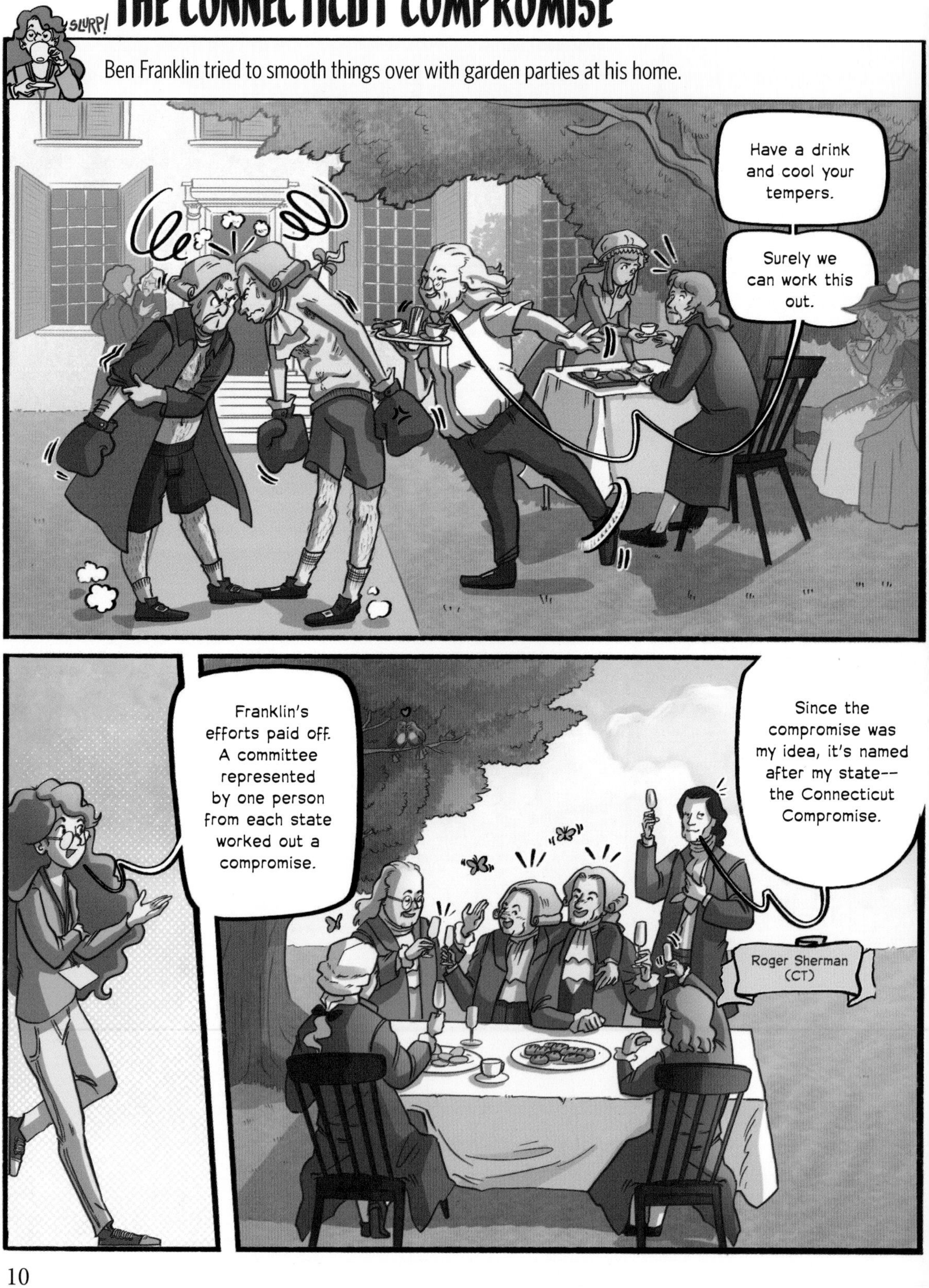
SLURP!
Ben Franklin tried to smooth things over with garden parties at his home.
Have a drink and cool your tempers.
Surely we can work this out.
Franklin's efforts paid off. A committee represented by one person from each state worked out a compromise.
Since the compromise was my idea, it's named after my state-- the Connecticut Compromise.
Roger Sherman (CT)

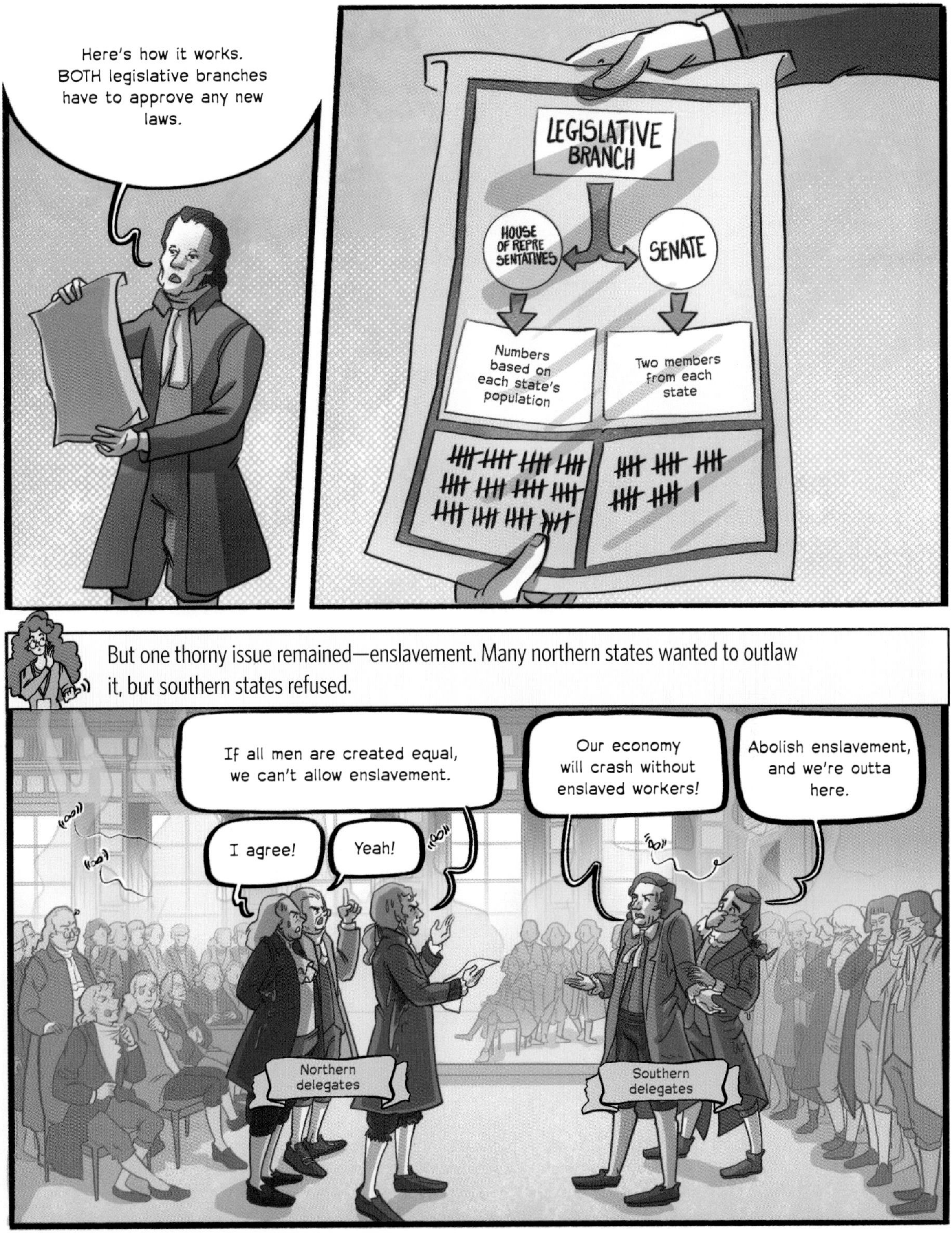
Here's how it works. BOTH legislative branches have to approve any new laws.
LEGISLATIVE BRANCH
HOUSE OF REPRE SENTATIVES
SENATE
Numbers based on each state's population
Two members from each state
But one thorny issue remained—enslavement. Many northern states wanted to outlaw it, but southern states refused.
If all men are created equal, we can't allow enslavement.
I agree!
Yeah!
Our economy will crash without enslaved workers!
Abolish enslavement, and we're outta here.
Northern delegates
Southern delegates

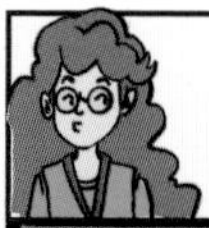

Many of the delegates at the convention, including George Washington, were enslavers. The anti-enslavement delegates felt stuck between a rock and a hard place.

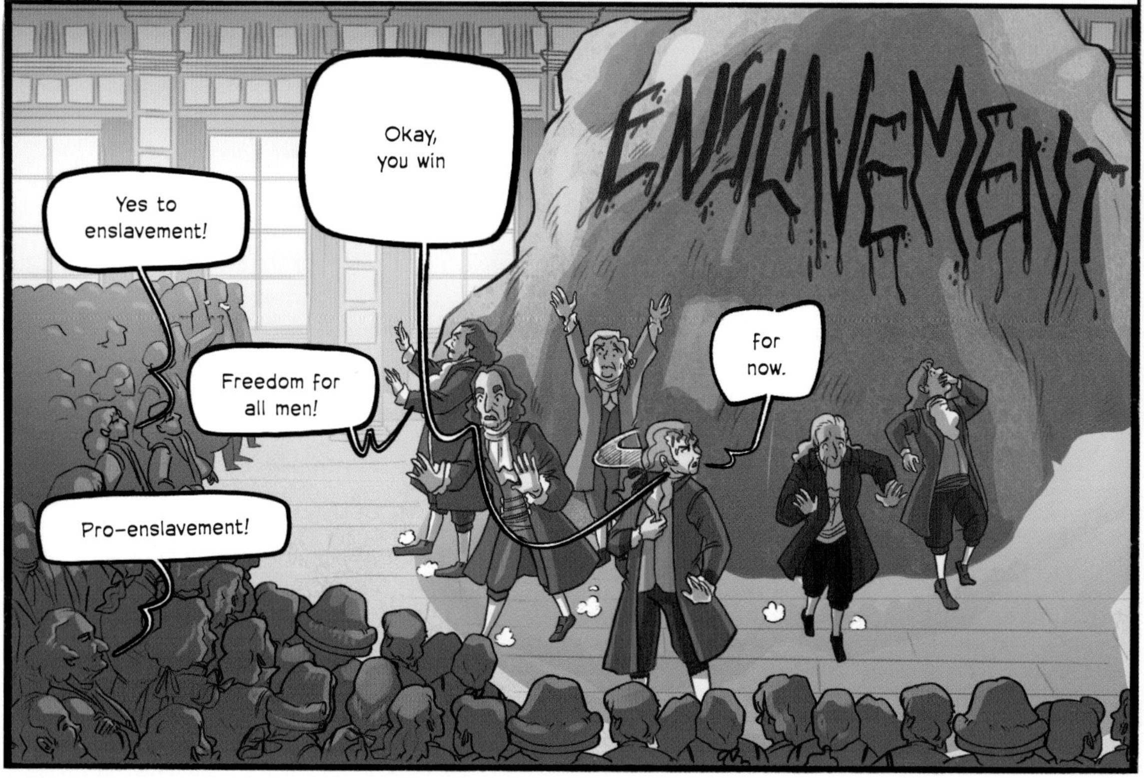
Yes to enslavement!
Okay, you win
ENSLAVEMENT
Freedom for all men!
For now.
Pro-enslavement!

In 1787, there were more than 600,000 enslaved people living in the U.S., mostly in the South. Owners of large farms there ran them as enslaved labor operations.

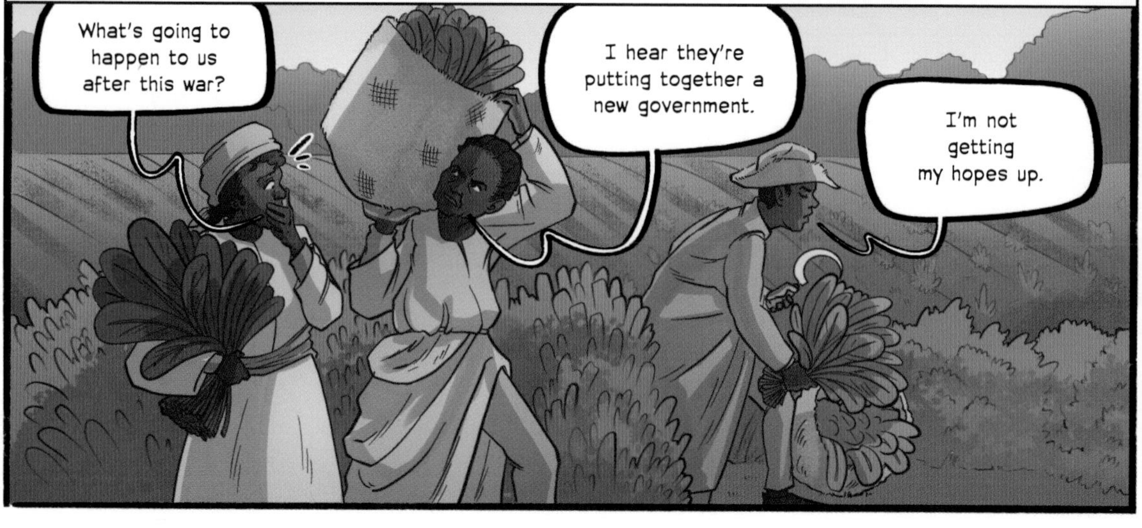
What's going to happen to us after this war?
I hear they're putting together a new government.
I'm not getting my hopes up.

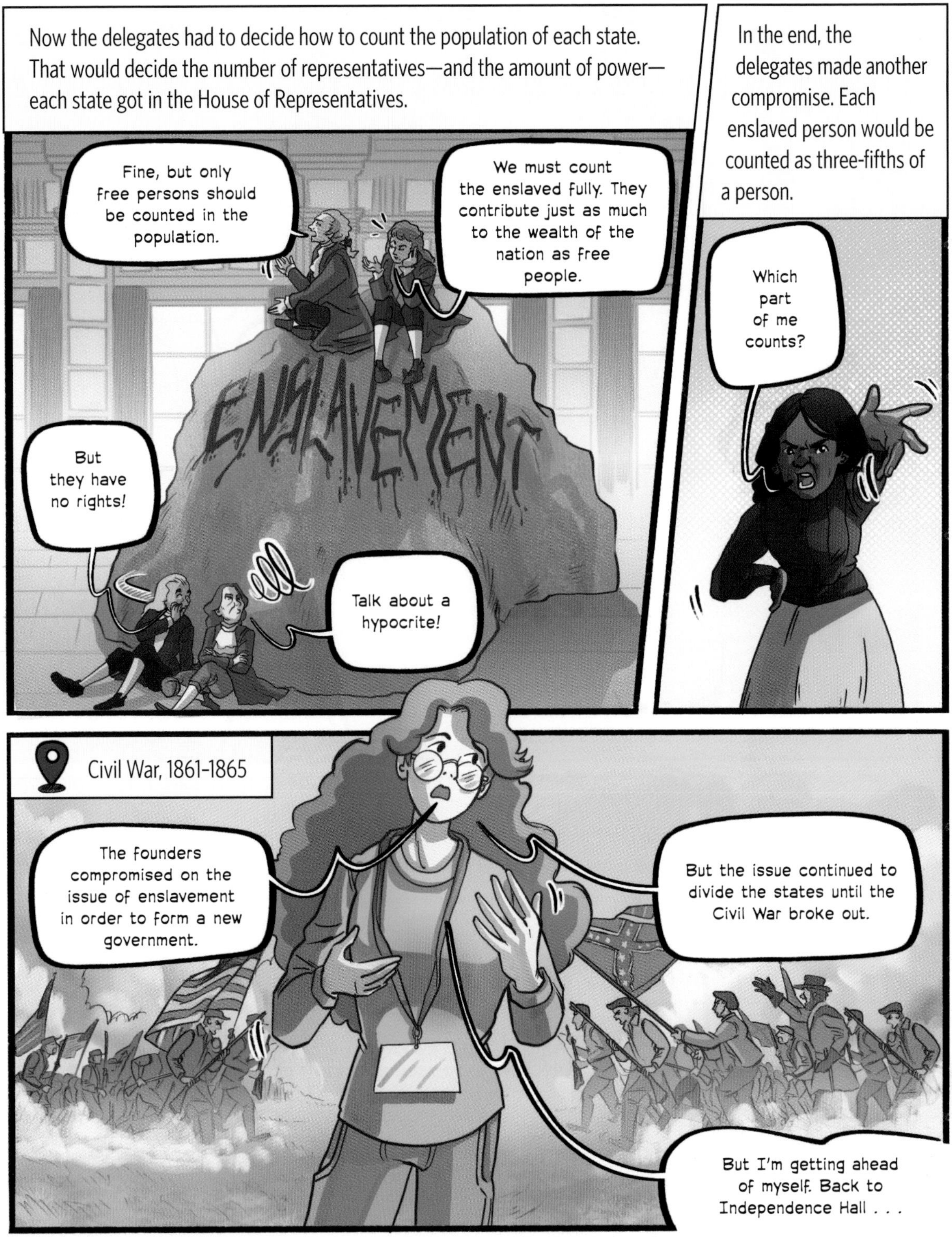
Now the delegates had to decide how to count the population of each state. That would decide the number of representatives—and the amount of power—each state got in the House of Representatives.
Fine, but only free persons should be counted in the population.
We must count the enslaved fully. They contribute just as much to the wealth of the nation as free people.
ENSLAVEMENT
But they have no rights!
Talk about a hypocrite!
In the end, the delegates made another compromise. Each enslaved person would be counted as three-fifths of a person.
Which part of me counts?
Civil War, 1861–1865
The founders compromised on the issue of enslavement in order to form a new government.
But the issue continued to divide the states until the Civil War broke out.
But I'm getting ahead of myself. Back to Independence Hall . . .

CHAPTER THREE: EXECUTIVE DECISIONS

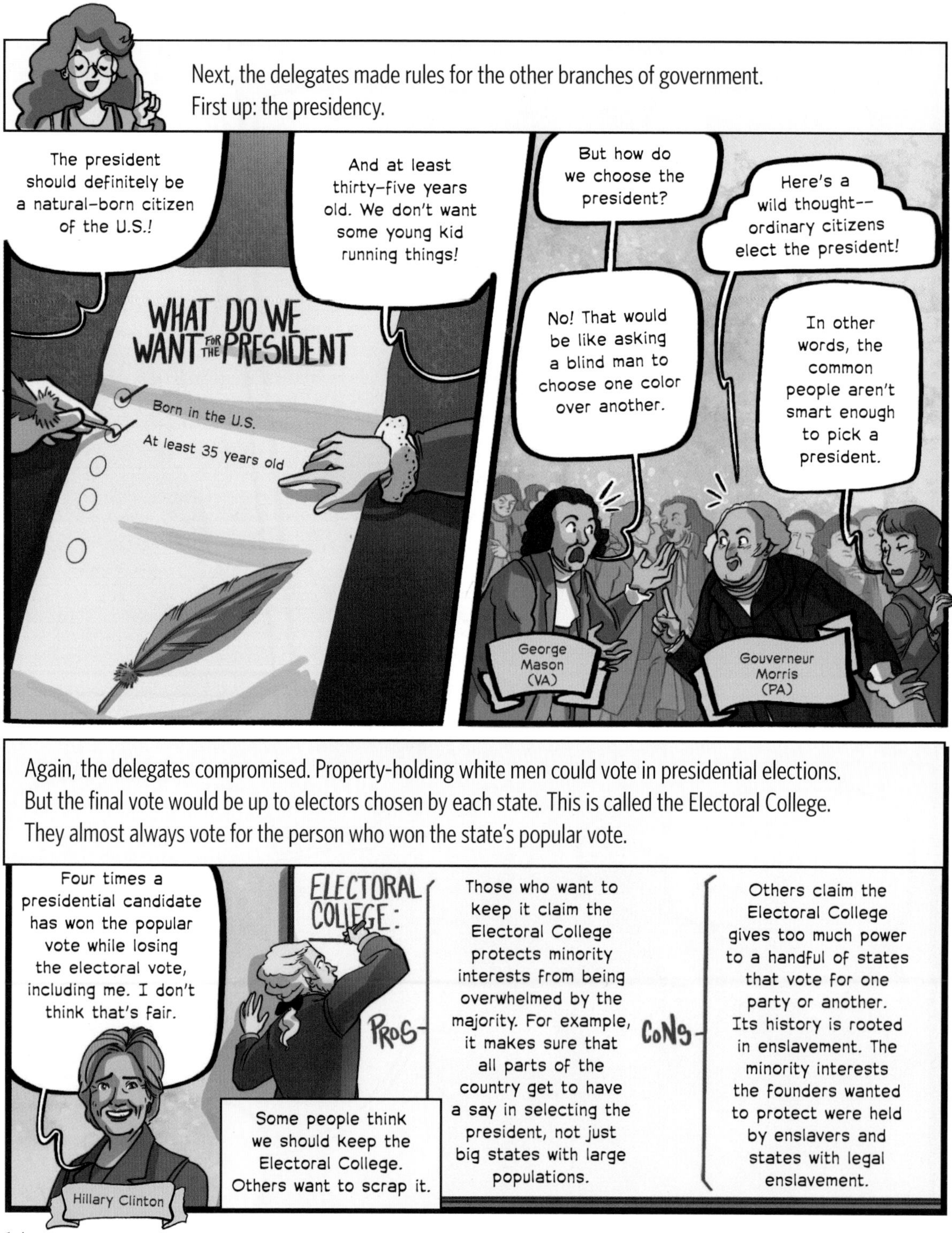

Next, the delegates made rules for the other branches of government. First up: the presidency.
The president should definitely be a natural-born citizen of the U.S.!
And at least thirty-five years old. We don't want some young kid running things!
WHAT DO WE WANT FOR THE PRESIDENT
Born in the U.S.
At least 35 years old
But how do we choose the president?
Here's a wild thought--ordinary citizens elect the president!
No! That would be like asking a blind man to choose one color over another.
In other words, the common people aren't smart enough to pick a president.
George Mason (VA)
Gouverneur Morris (PA)
Again, the delegates compromised. Property-holding white men could vote in presidential elections. But the final vote would be up to electors chosen by each state. This is called the Electoral College. They almost always vote for the person who won the state's popular vote.
Four times a presidential candidate has won the popular vote while losing the electoral vote, including me. I don't think that's fair.
Hillary Clinton
ELECTORAL COLLEGE:
PROS-
Those who want to keep it claim the Electoral College protects minority interests from being overwhelmed by the majority. For example, it makes sure that all parts of the country get to have a say in selecting the president, not just big states with large populations.
CONS-
Others claim the Electoral College gives too much power to a handful of states that vote for one party or another. Its history is rooted in enslavement. The minority interests the founders wanted to protect were held by enslavers and states with legal enslavement.
Some people think we should keep the Electoral College. Others want to scrap it.

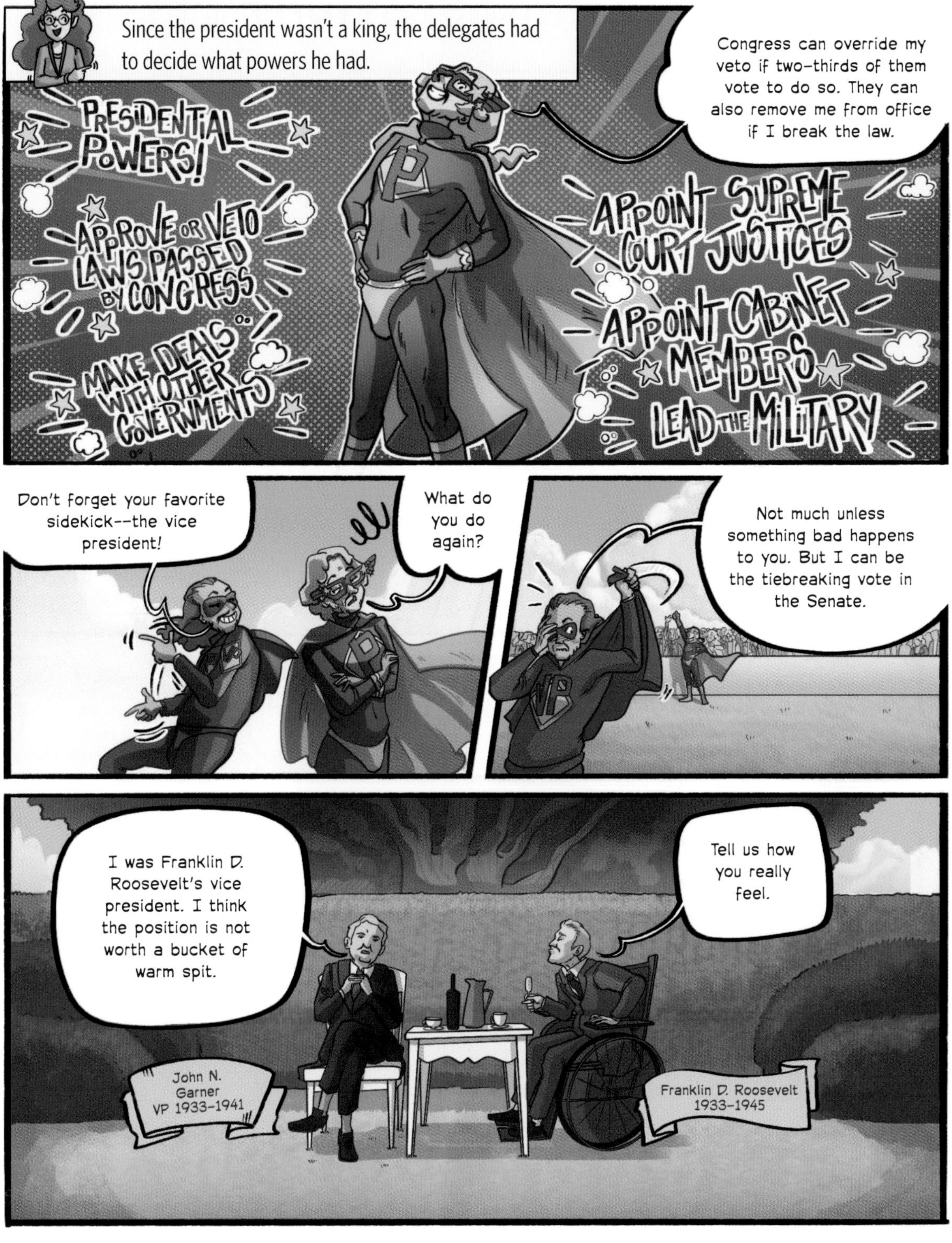
Since the president wasn't a king, the delegates had to decide what powers he had.
Congress can override my veto if two-thirds of them vote to do so. They can also remove me from office if I break the law.
PRESIDENTIAL POWERS!
APPROVE OR VETO LAWS PASSED BY CONGRESS
MAKE DEALS WITH OTHER GOVERNMENTS
APPOINT SUPREME COURT JUSTICES
APPOINT CABINET MEMBERS
LEAD THE MILITARY
Don't forget your favorite sidekick--the vice president!
What do you do again?
Not much unless something bad happens to you. But I can be the tiebreaking vote in the Senate.
I was Franklin D. Roosevelt's vice president. I think the position is not worth a bucket of warm spit.
Tell us how you really feel.
John N. Garner VP 1933–1941
Franklin D. Roosevelt 1933–1945

CHAPTER FOUR: RULES AND REGULATIONS

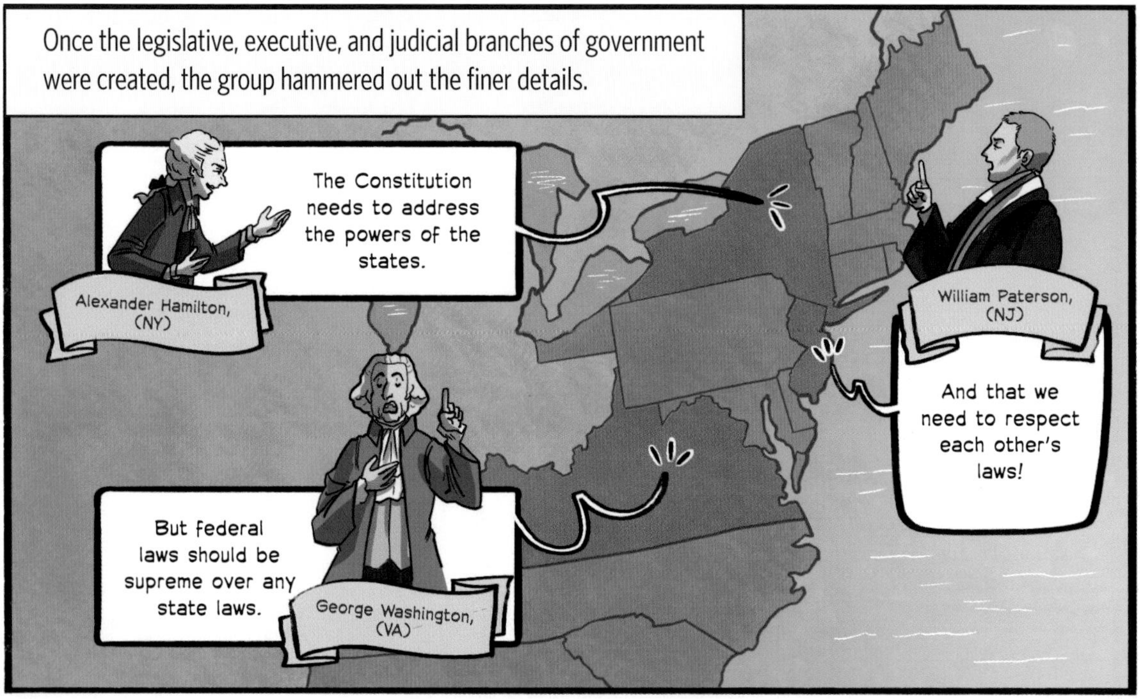
Once the legislative, executive, and judicial branches of government were created, the group hammered out the finer details.
The Constitution needs to address the powers of the states.
Alexander Hamilton, (NY)
William Paterson, (NJ)
And that we need to respect each other's laws!
But federal laws should be supreme over any state laws.
George Washington, (VA)

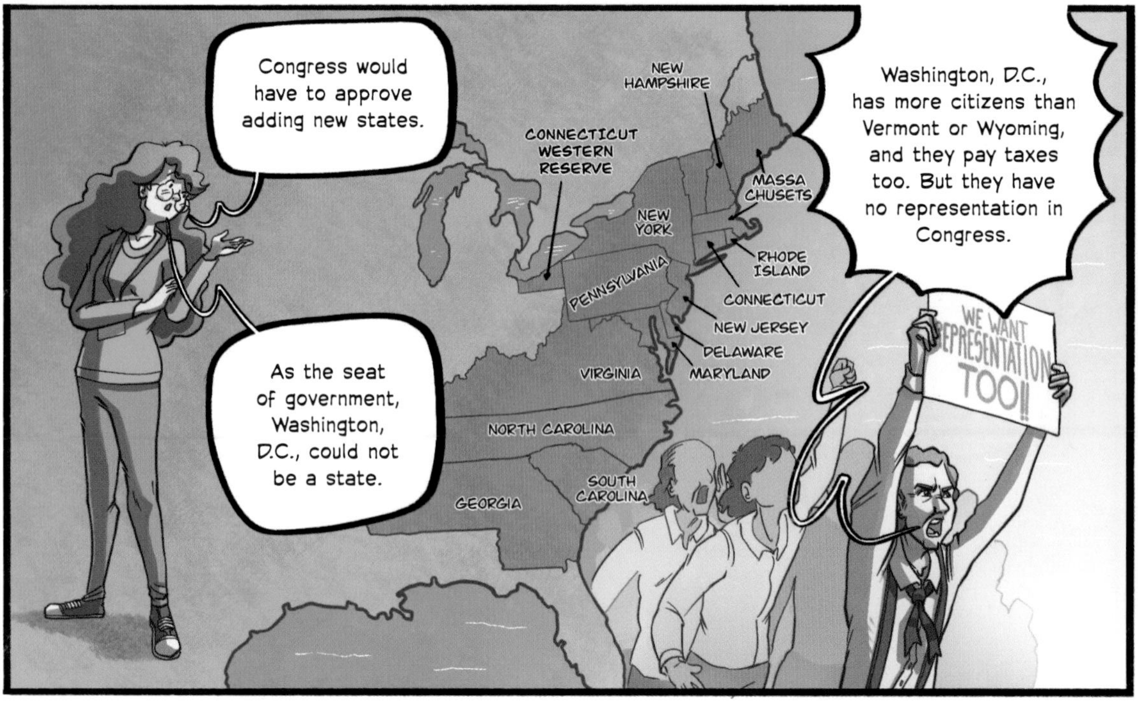
Congress would have to approve adding new states.
As the seat of government, Washington, D.C., could not be a state.
NEW HAMPSHIRE
CONNECTICUT WESTERN RESERVE
MASSA CHUSETS
NEW YORK
RHODE ISLAND
PENNSYLVANIA
CONNECTICUT
NEW JERSEY
DELAWARE
MARYLAND
VIRGINIA
NORTH CAROLINA
SOUTH CAROLINA
GEORGIA
Washington, D.C., has more citizens than Vermont or Wyoming, and they pay taxes too. But they have no representation in Congress.
WE WANT REPRESENTATION TOO!!

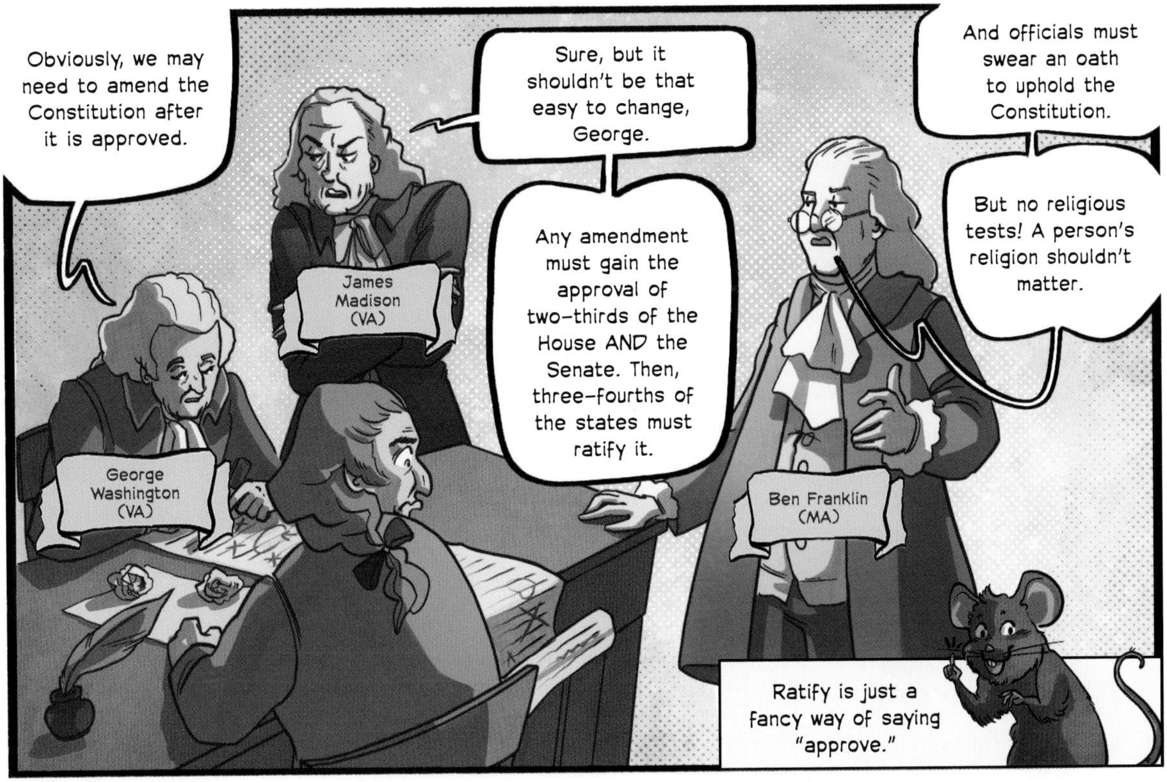
Obviously, we may need to amend the Constitution after it is approved.
Sure, but it shouldn't be that easy to change, George.
Any amendment must gain the approval of two-thirds of the House AND the Senate. Then, three-fourths of the states must ratify it.
James Madison (VA)
George Washington (VA)
And officials must swear an oath to uphold the Constitution.
But no religious tests! A person's religion shouldn't matter.
Ben Franklin (MA)
Ratify is just a fancy way of saying "approve."

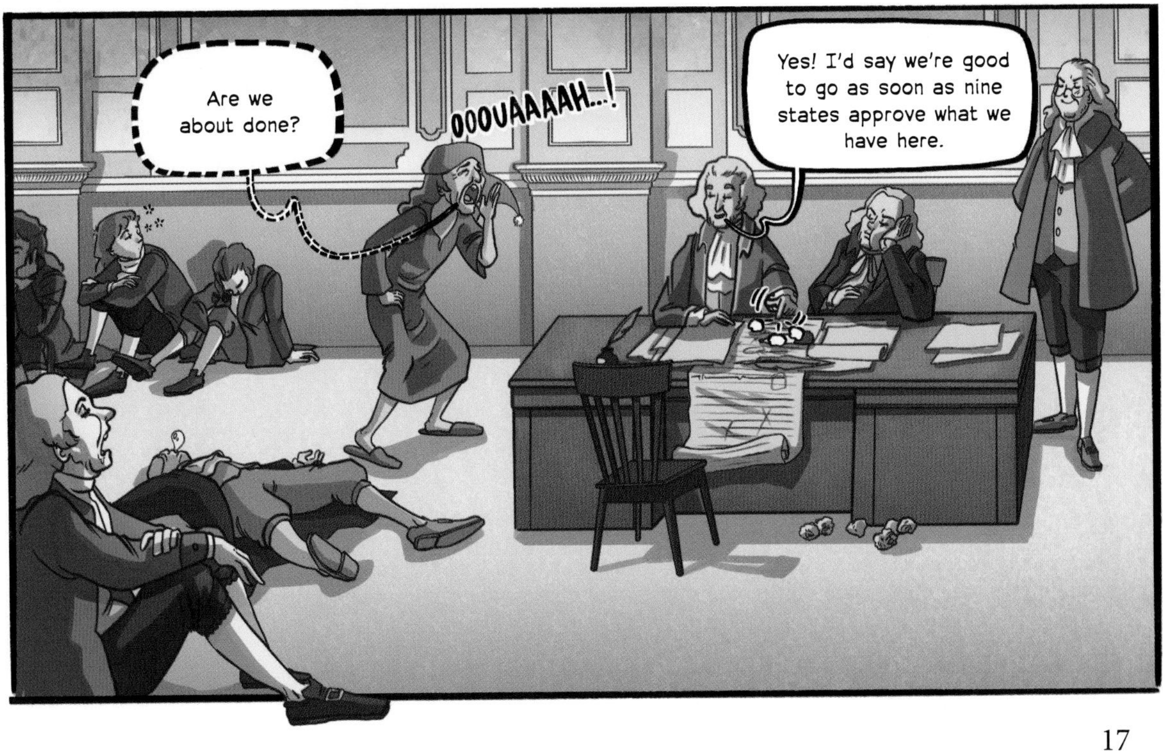
Are we about done?
OOOUAAAAH..!
Yes! I'd say we're good to go as soon as nine states approve what we have here.

CHAPTER FIVE: GETTING THE WORD OUT

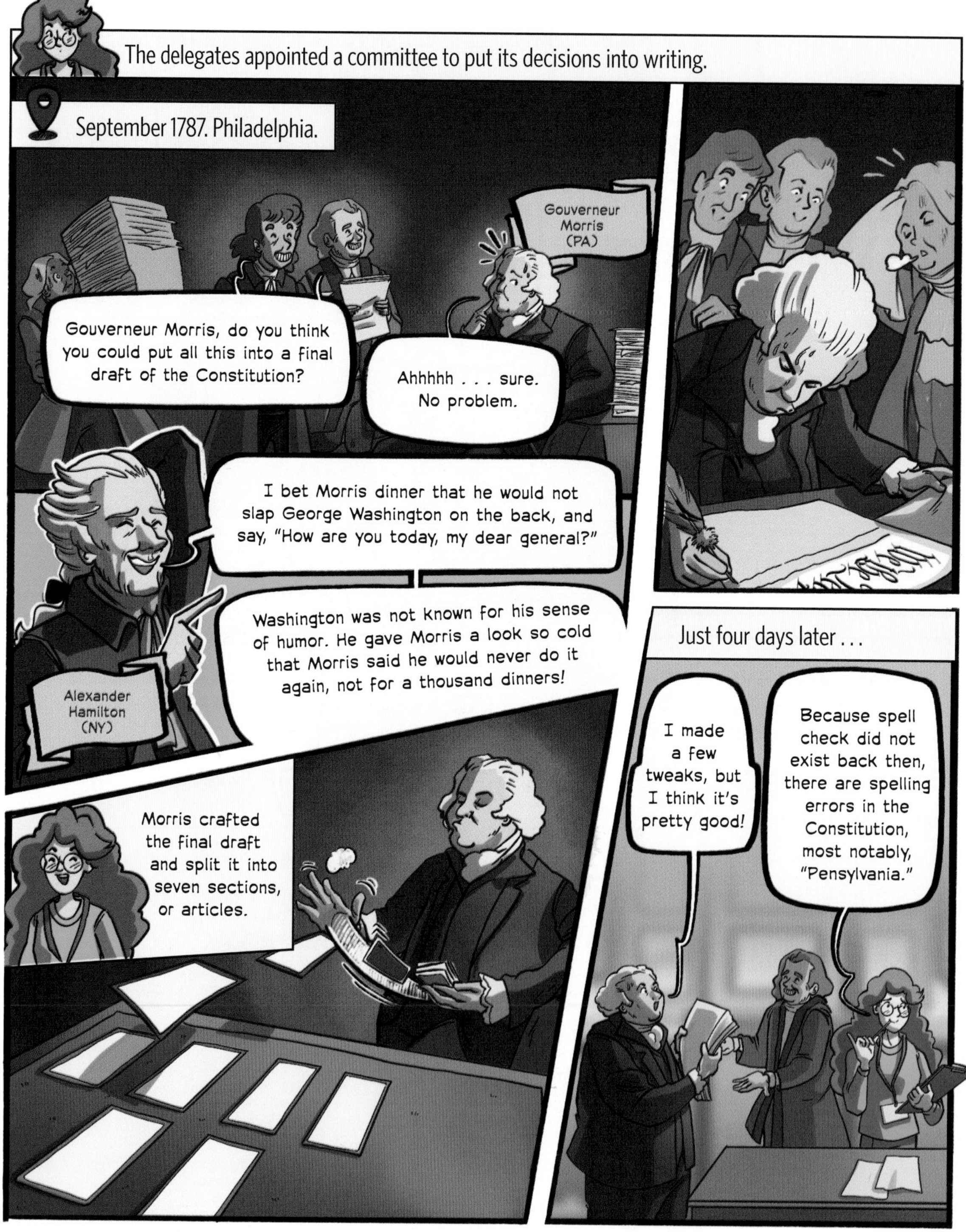

The delegates appointed a committee to put its decisions into writing.
September 1787. Philadelphia.
Gouverneur Morris (PA)
Gouverneur Morris, do you think you could put all this into a final draft of the Constitution?
Ahhhhh . . . sure. No problem.
I bet Morris dinner that he would not slap George Washington on the back, and say, "How are you today, my dear general?"
Washington was not known for his sense of humor. He gave Morris a look so cold that Morris said he would never do it again, not for a thousand dinners!
Alexander Hamilton (NY)
Morris crafted the final draft and split it into seven sections, or articles.
Just four days later . . .
I made a few tweaks, but I think it's pretty good!
Because spell check did not exist back then, there are spelling errors in the Constitution, most notably, "Pensylvania."

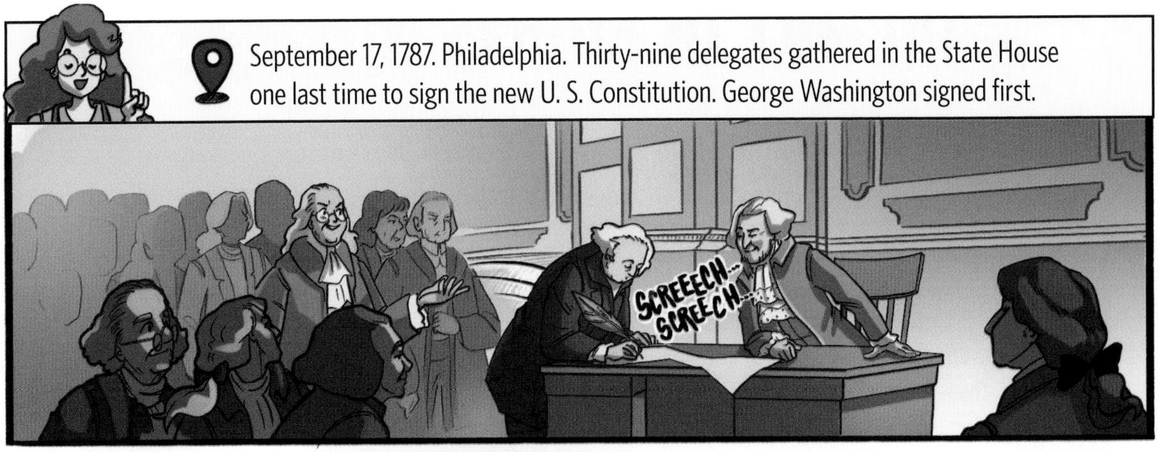

September 17, 1787. Philadelphia. Thirty-nine delegates gathered in the State House one last time to sign the new U. S. Constitution. George Washington signed first.
SCREEECH...
SCREECH...

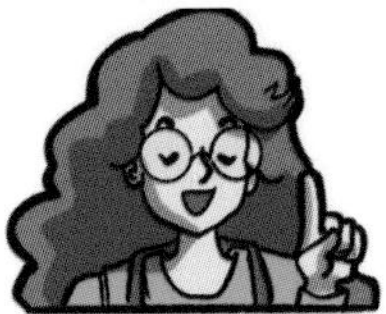

FEDERALIST PAPERS

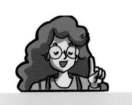

Alexander Hamilton, James Madison, and John Jay wrote 85 essays urging New Yorkers to ratify the Constitution. These essays became known as the Federalist Papers and are used to this day to help us interpret the intentions of the framers of the U.S. Constitution.

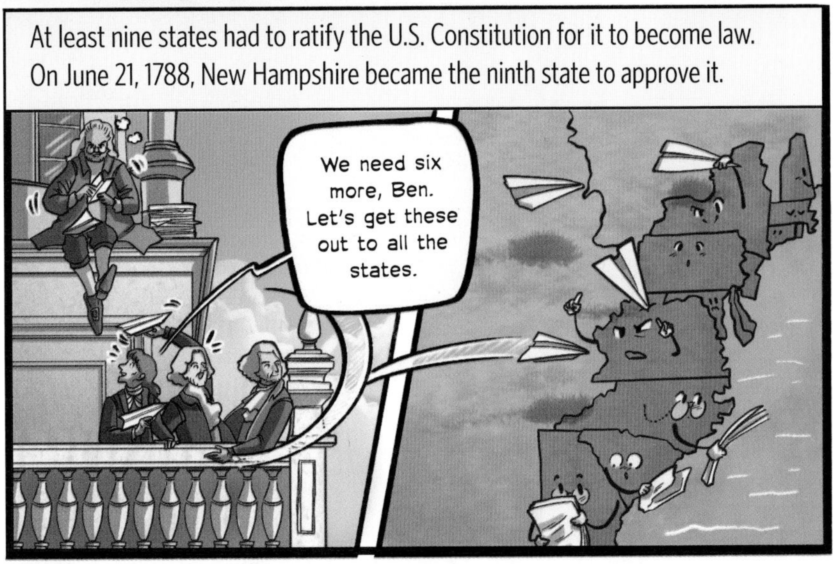

At least nine states had to ratify the U.S. Constitution for it to become law. On June 21, 1788, New Hampshire became the ninth state to approve it.
We need six more, Ben. Let's get these out to all the states.

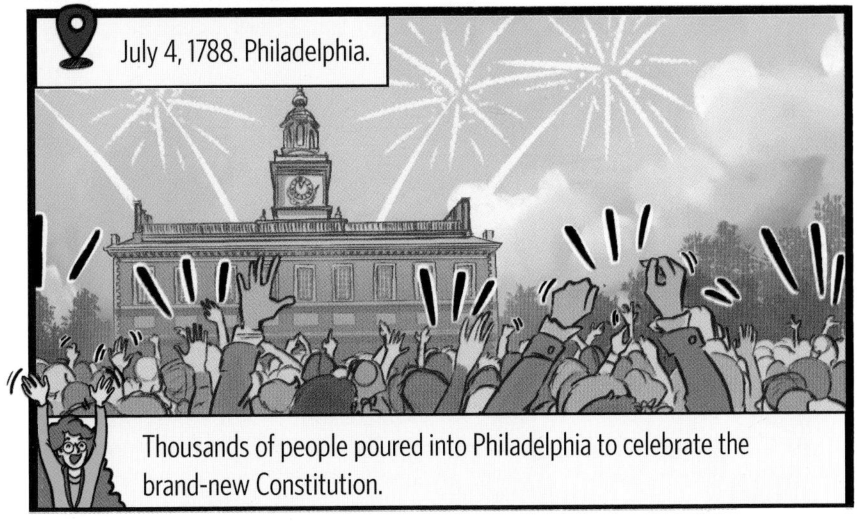

July 4, 1788. Philadelphia.
Thousands of people poured into Philadelphia to celebrate the brand-new Constitution.

CHAPTER SIX: THE BILL OF RIGHTS

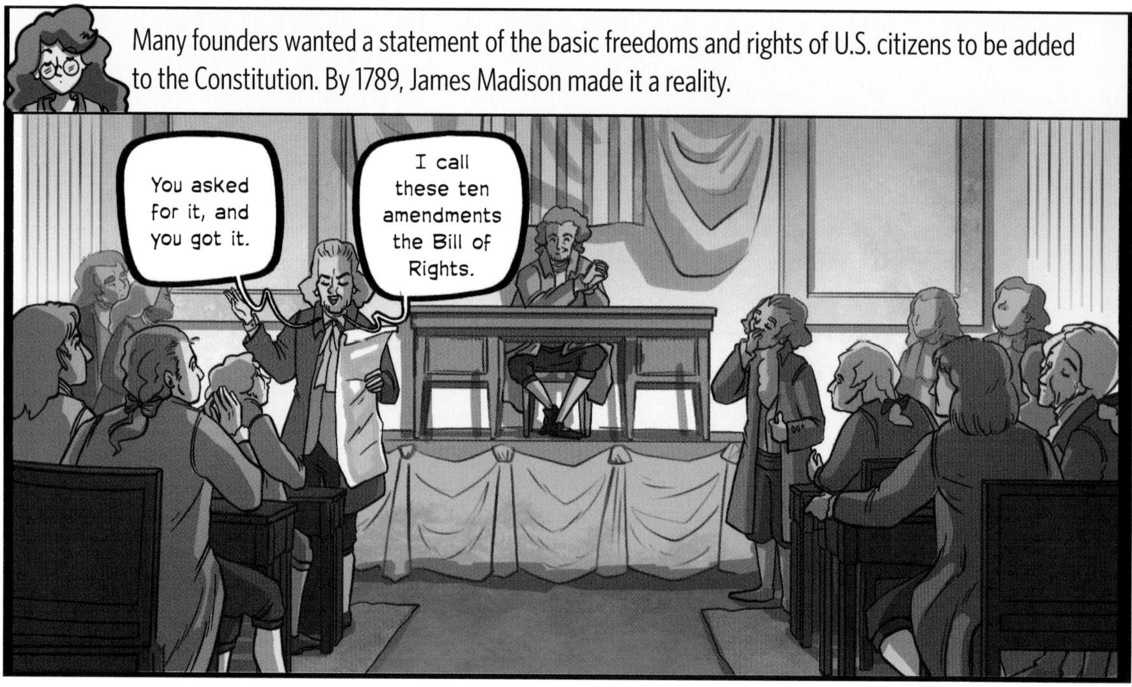
Many founders wanted a statement of the basic freedoms and rights of U.S. citizens to be added to the Constitution. By 1789, James Madison made it a reality.
You asked for it, and you got it.
I call these ten amendments the Bill of Rights.

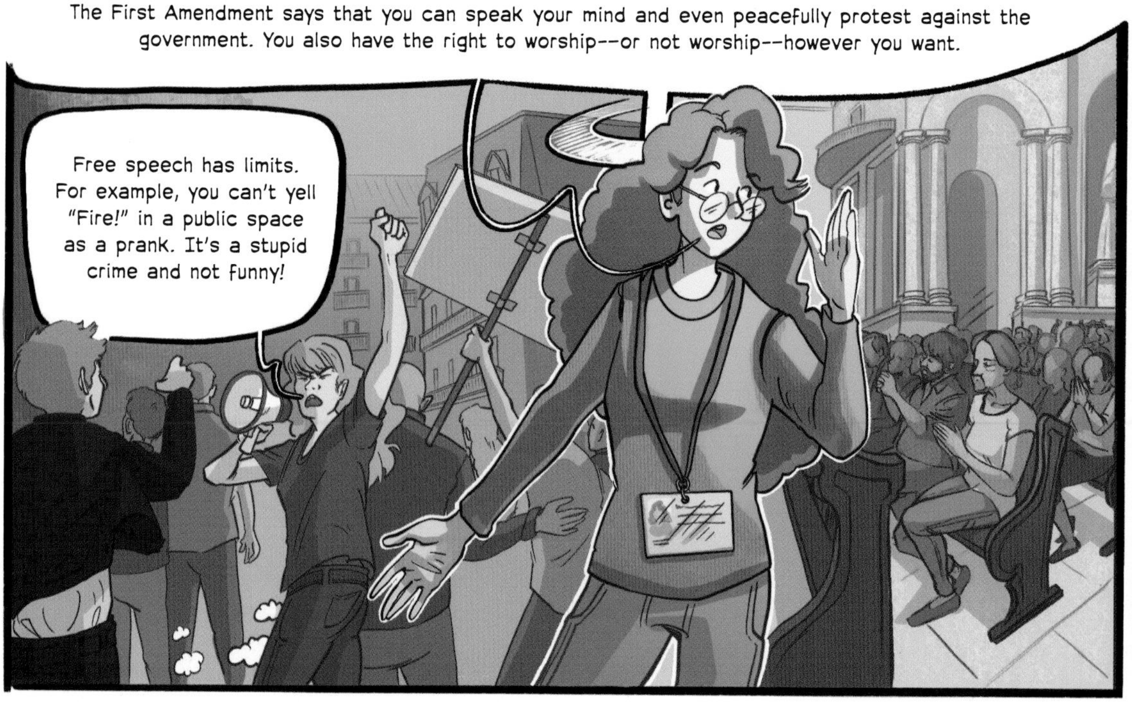
The First Amendment says that you can speak your mind and even peacefully protest against the government. You also have the right to worship--or not worship--however you want.
Free speech has limits. For example, you can't yell "Fire!" in a public space as a prank. It's a stupid crime and not funny!

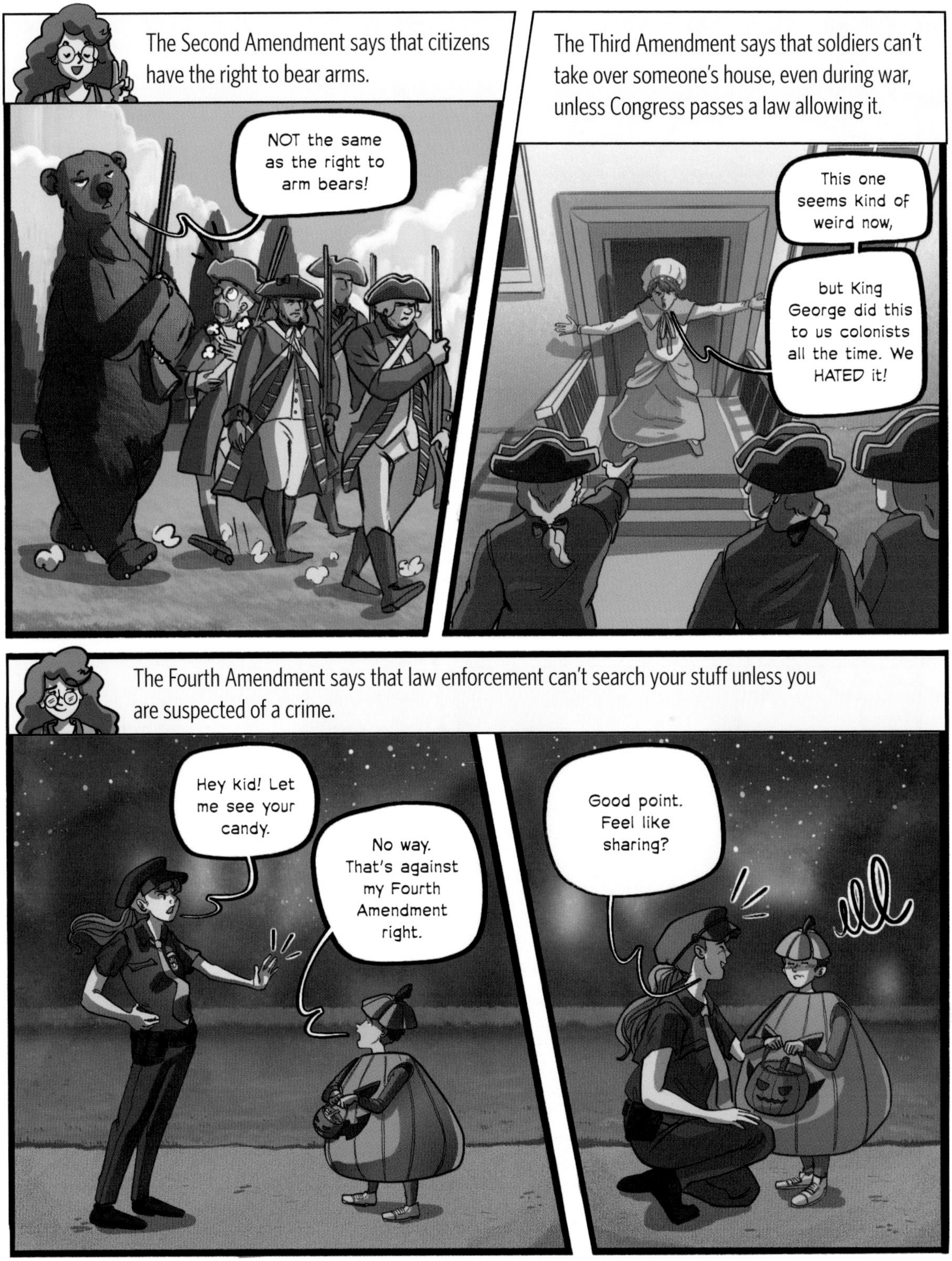
The Second Amendment says that citizens have the right to bear arms.
NOT the same as the right to arm bears!
The Third Amendment says that soldiers can't take over someone's house, even during war, unless Congress passes a law allowing it.
This one seems kind of weird now,
but King George did this to us colonists all the time. We HATED it!
The Fourth Amendment says that law enforcement can't search your stuff unless you are suspected of a crime.
Hey kid! Let me see your candy.
No way. That's against my Fourth Amendment right.
Good point. Feel like sharing?

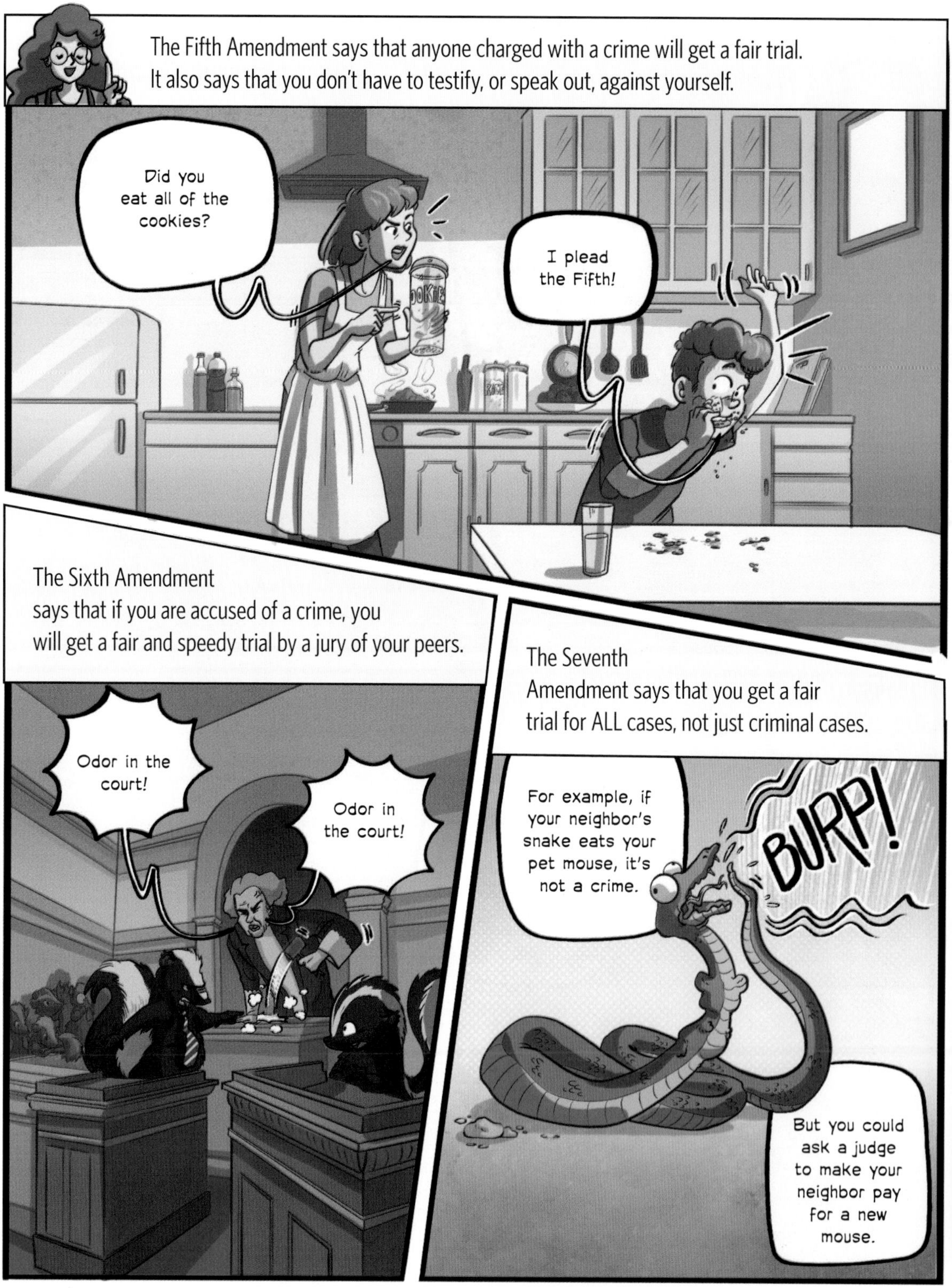
The Fifth Amendment says that anyone charged with a crime will get a fair trial. It also says that you don't have to testify, or speak out, against yourself.
Did you eat all of the cookies?
I plead the Fifth!
The Sixth Amendment says that if you are accused of a crime, you will get a fair and speedy trial by a jury of your peers.
Odor in the court!
Odor in the court!
The Seventh Amendment says that you get a fair trial for ALL cases, not just criminal cases.
For example, if your neighbor's snake eats your pet mouse, it's not a crime.
BURP!
But you could ask a judge to make your neighbor pay for a new mouse.

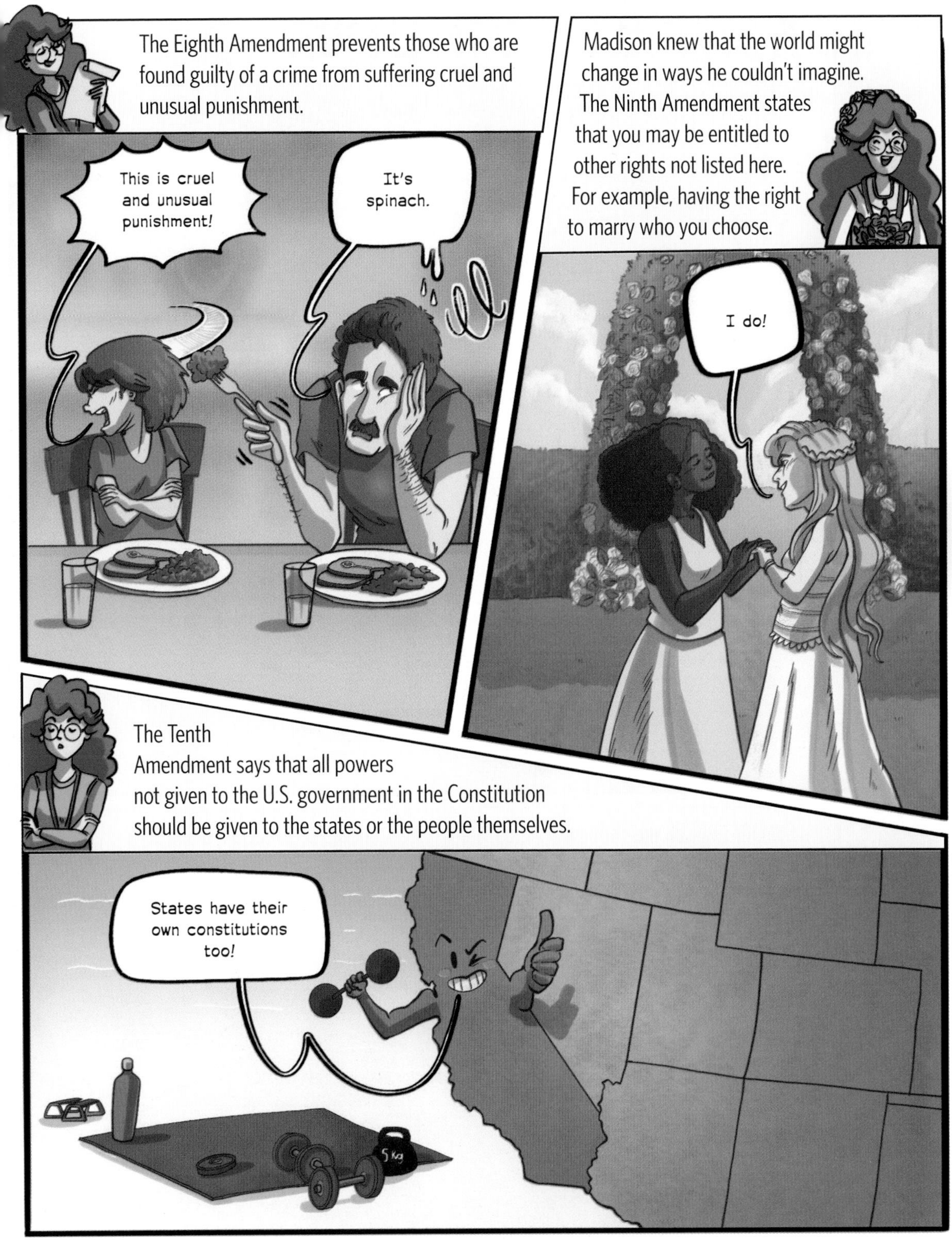
The Eighth Amendment prevents those who are found guilty of a crime from suffering cruel and unusual punishment.
This is cruel and unusual punishment!
It's spinach.
Madison knew that the world might change in ways he couldn't imagine. The Ninth Amendment states that you may be entitled to other rights not listed here. For example, having the right to marry who you choose.
I do!
The Tenth Amendment says that all powers not given to the U.S. government in the Constitution should be given to the states or the people themselves.
States have their own constitutions too!
5 kg

CHAPTER SEVEN: A LIVING CONSTITUTION

The Bill of Rights was just the beginning. Many people have fought for amendments to the Constitution to ensure equal rights for all.

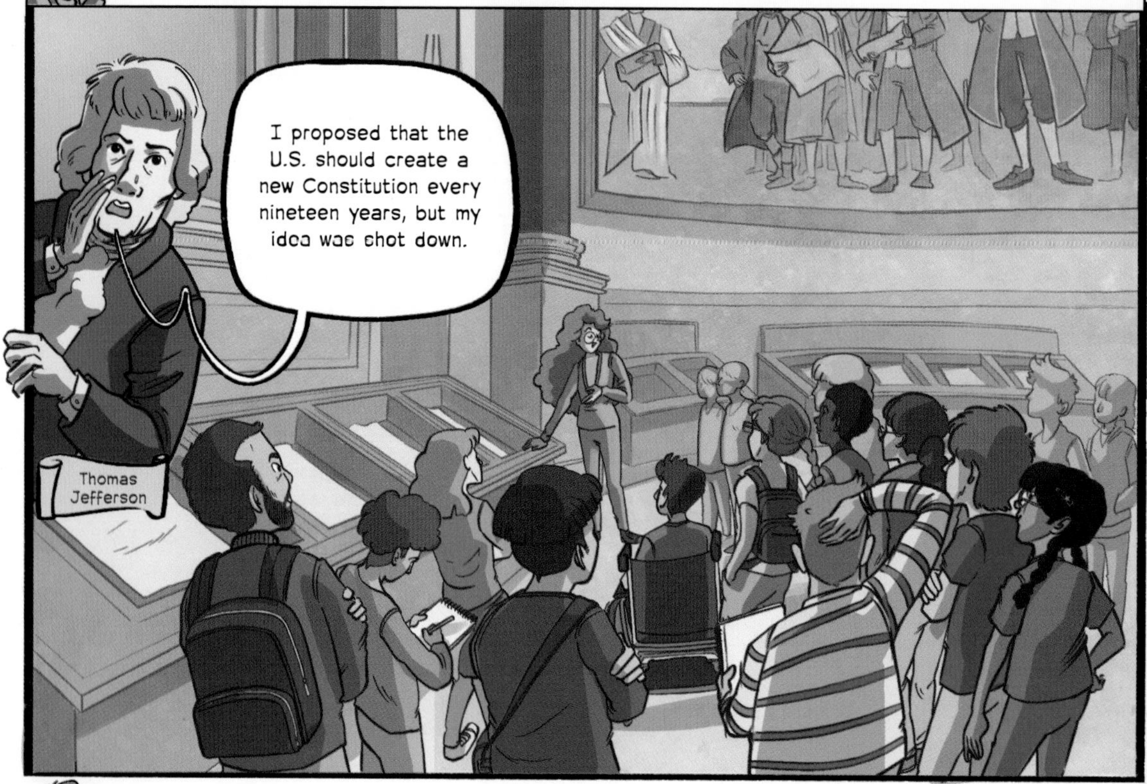
I proposed that the U.S. should create a new Constitution every nineteen years, but my idea was shot down.
Thomas Jefferson

Congress passed the Thirteenth Amendment on January 31, 1865. It abolished legal enslavement everywhere in the United States.

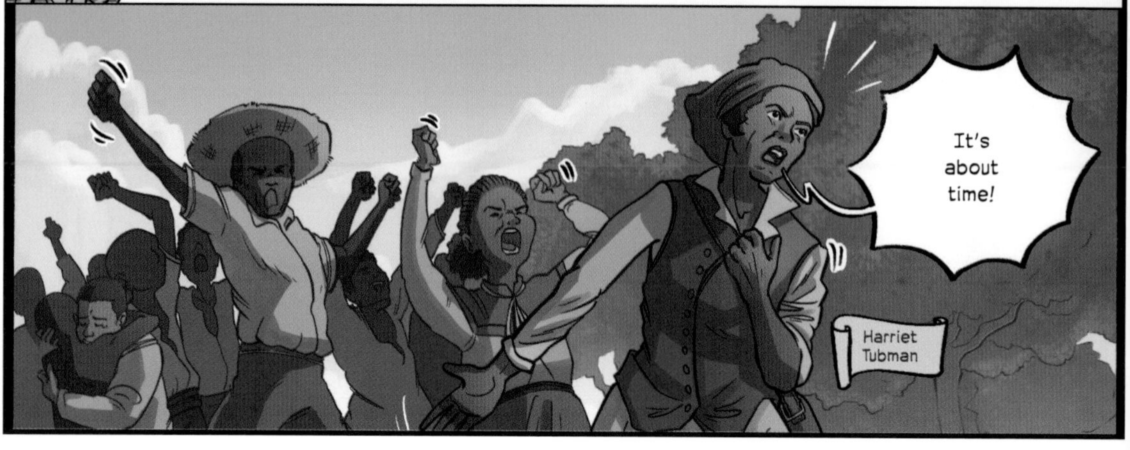
It's about time!
Harriet Tubman

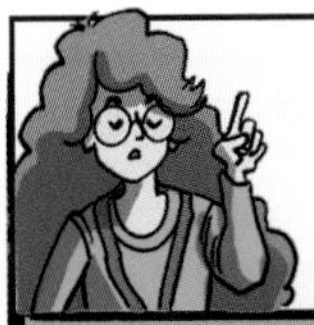

The Fourteenth Amendment was passed by Congress on June 13, 1866. It granted full citizenship to all people born in the U.S., including formerly enslaved people. Everyone should have equal protection under the law.

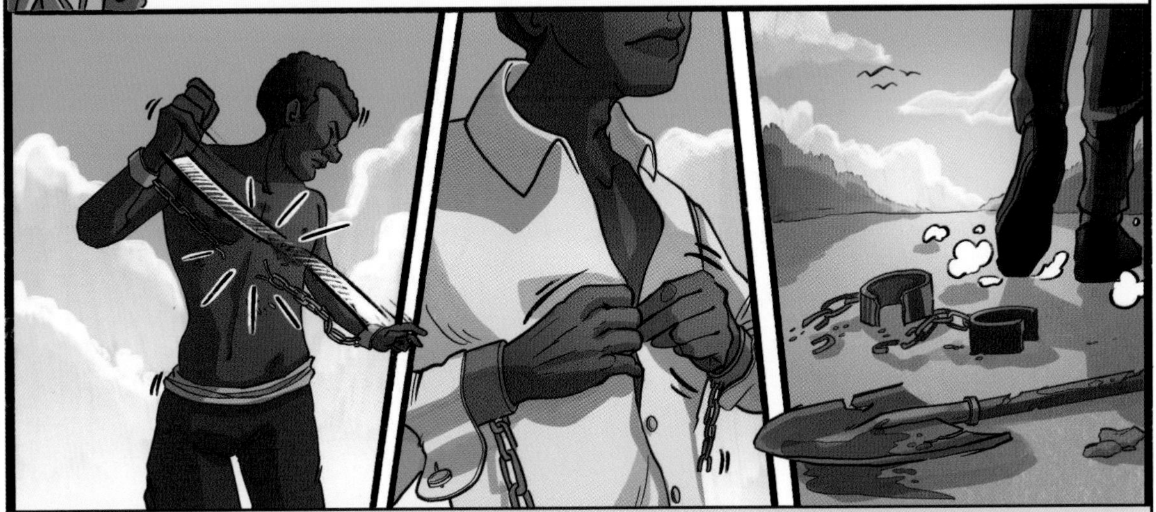

FACT!

The Fourteenth Amendment came after the Civil War. Some southern states passed laws to restrict the rights and freedoms of Black Americans. Before the Fourteenth Amendment, if you were jobless, you could be arrested and forced to work in a prison. It was just like being enslaved!

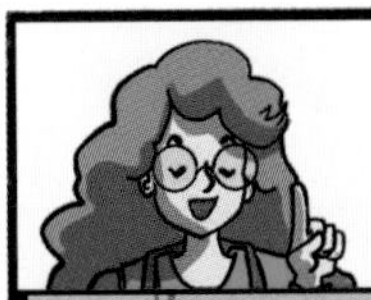

Congress passed the Fifteenth Amendment on February 26, 1869. It said that a U.S. citizen can't be denied the right to vote based on race, skin color, or whether they were once enslaved. But it said nothing about gender.

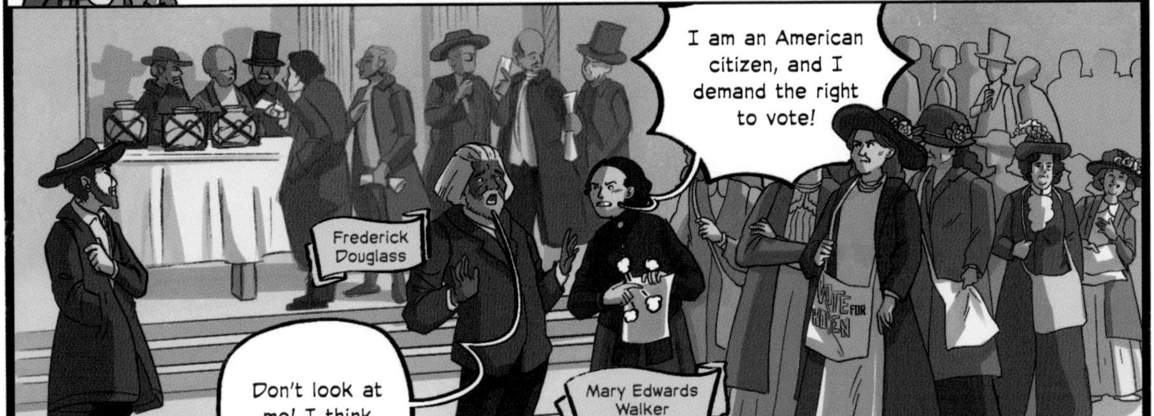
I am an American citizen, and I demand the right to vote!
Frederick Douglass
Mary Edwards Walker
Don't look at me! I think you're right.

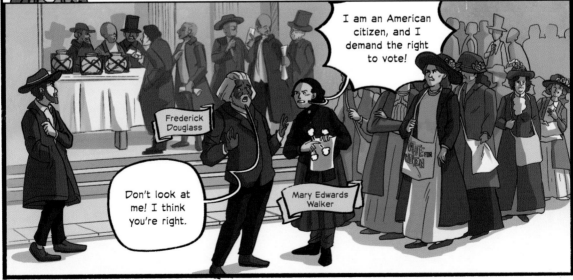

Women were finally granted the right to vote on June 4, 1919, with the passage of the Nineteenth Amendment.

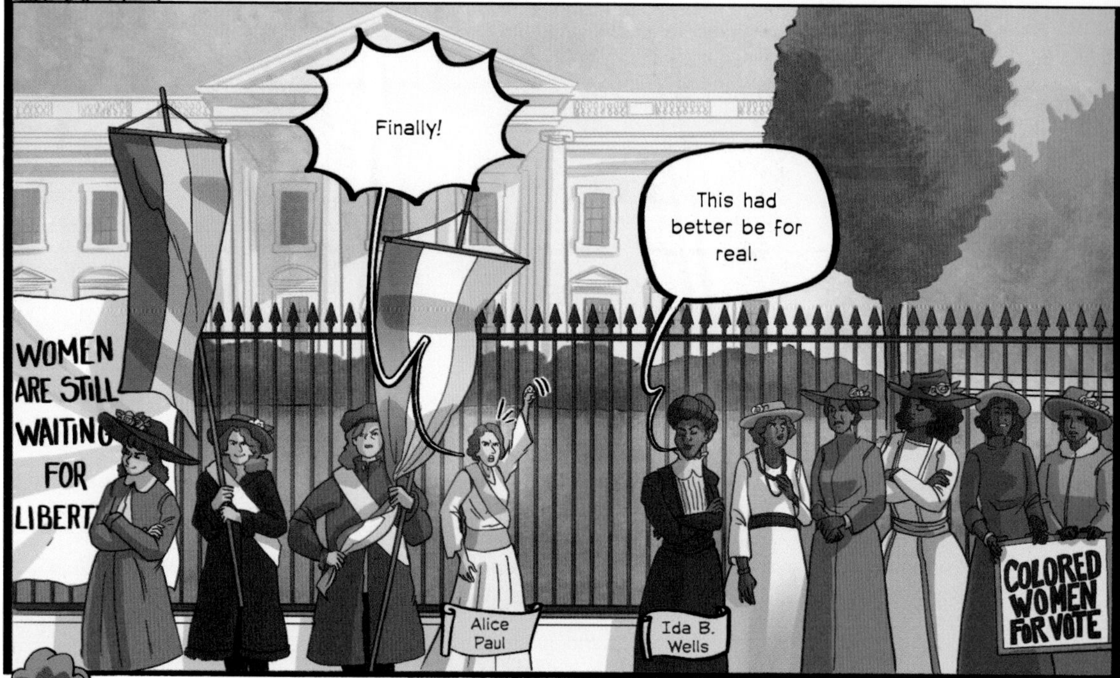
WOMEN ARE STILL WAITING FOR LIBERT
Finally!
This had better be for real.
Alice Paul
Ida B. Wells
COLORED WOMEN FOR VOTE

Some states still had poll taxes. This made voting more difficult for some people. Black people, in particular, were often paid less than white people.

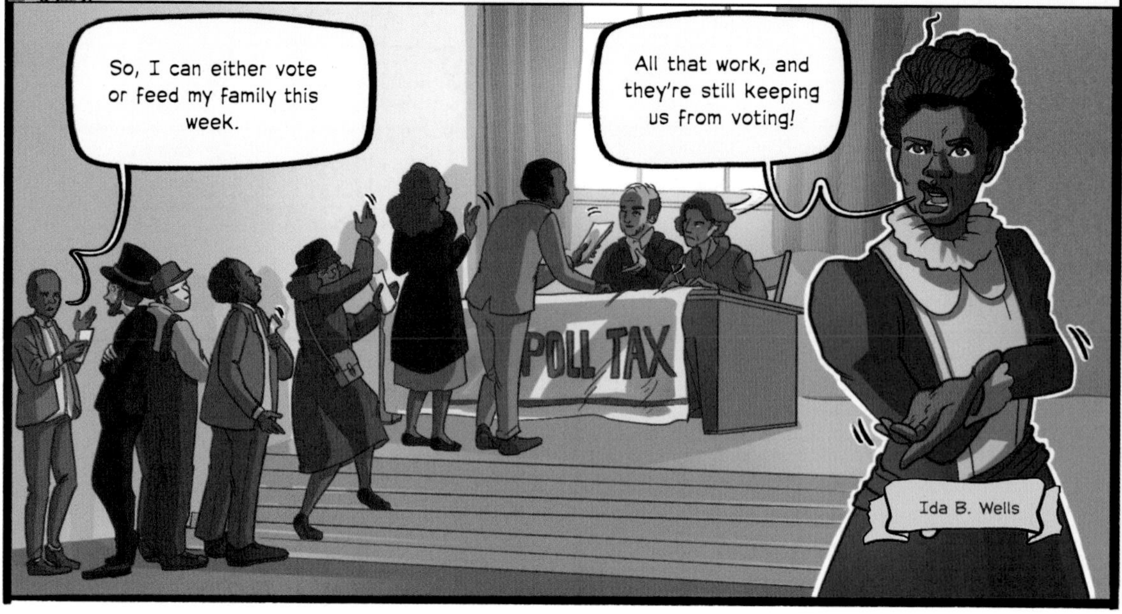
So, I can either vote or feed my family this week.
All that work, and they're still keeping us from voting!
POLL TAX
Ida B. Wells

The Twenty-fourth Amendment was passed on August 27, 1962. It said that you can't be denied the right to vote just because you can't afford to pay a tax at the polls.

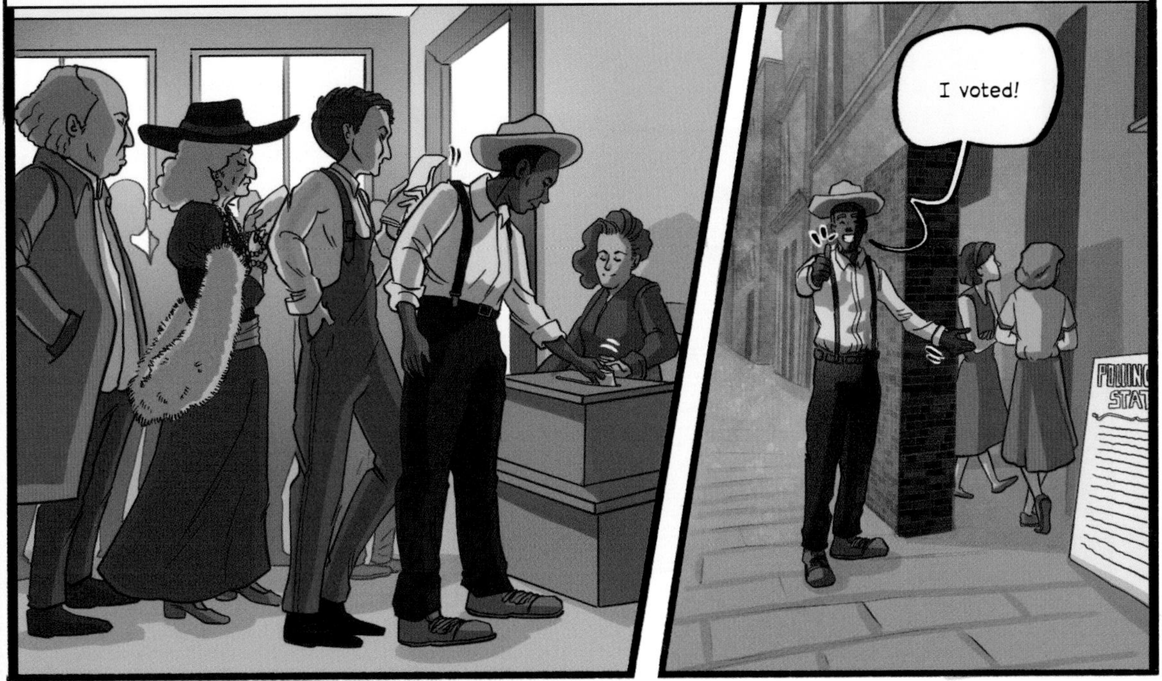
I voted!

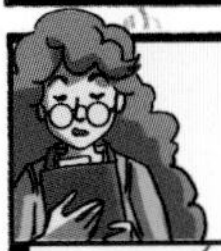

The Twenty-sixth Amendment was passed by Congress on March 23, 1971. It lowered the voting age from 21 to 18.

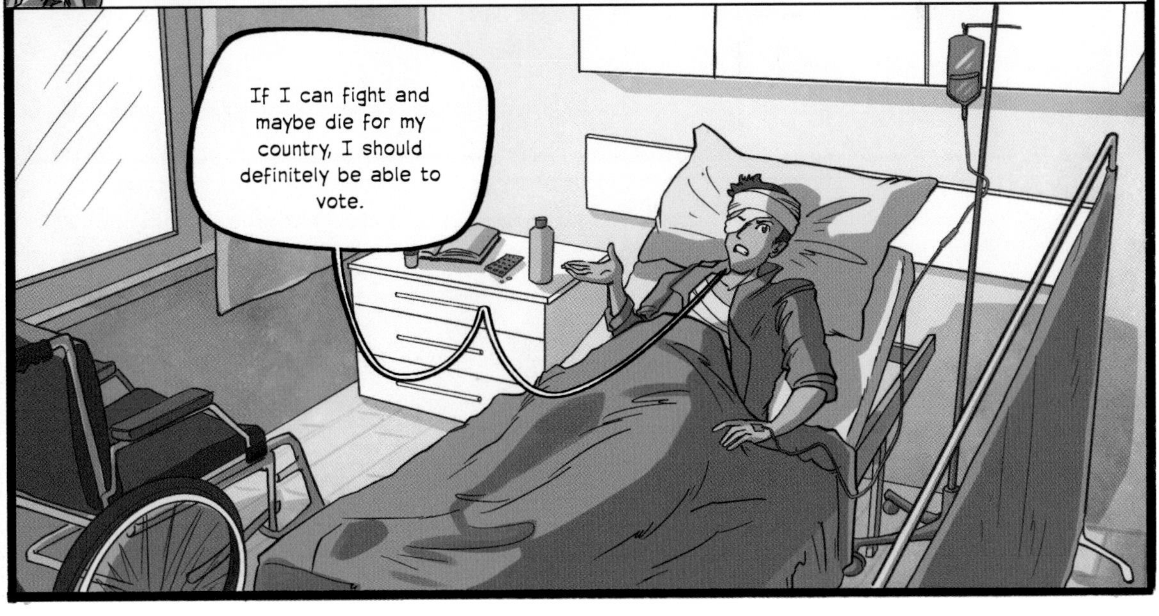
If I can fight and maybe die for my country, I should definitely be able to vote.

Today, we continue to debate what the Constitution has to tell us. About freedom of speech . . .

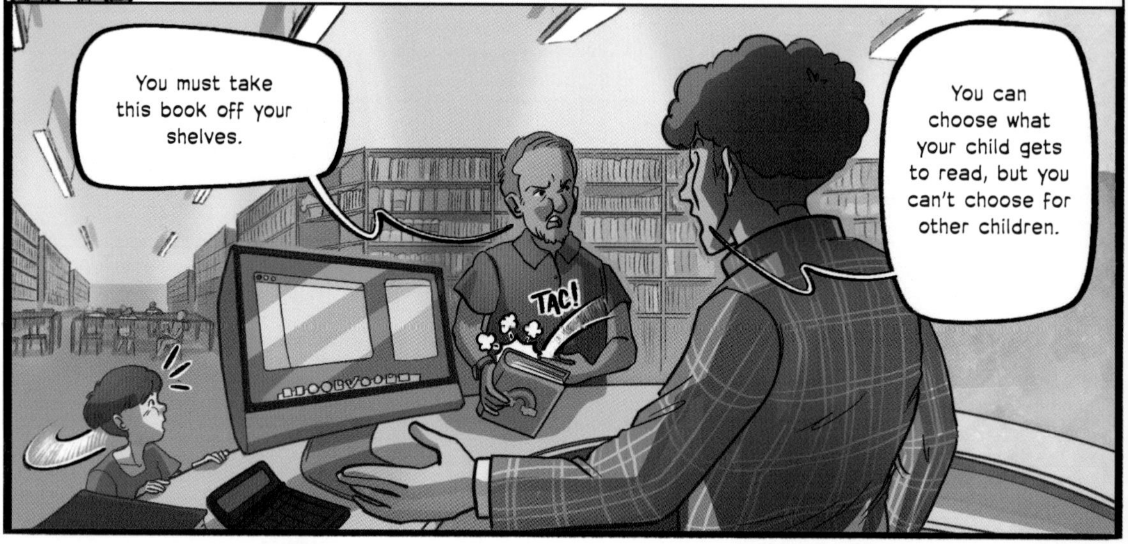

You must take this book off your shelves.
TAC!
You can choose what your child gets to read, but you can't choose for other children.

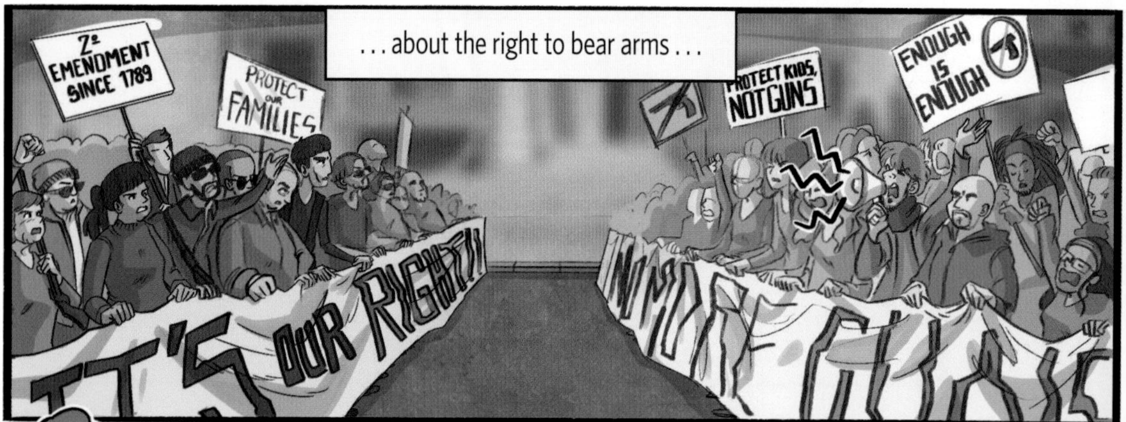

. . . about the right to bear arms . . .
2º EMENDMENT SINCE 1789
PROTECT OUR FAMILIES
PROTECT KIDS, NOT GUNS
ENOUGH IS ENOUGH

. . . or about whether the Constitution allows colleges to consider race when admitting students.

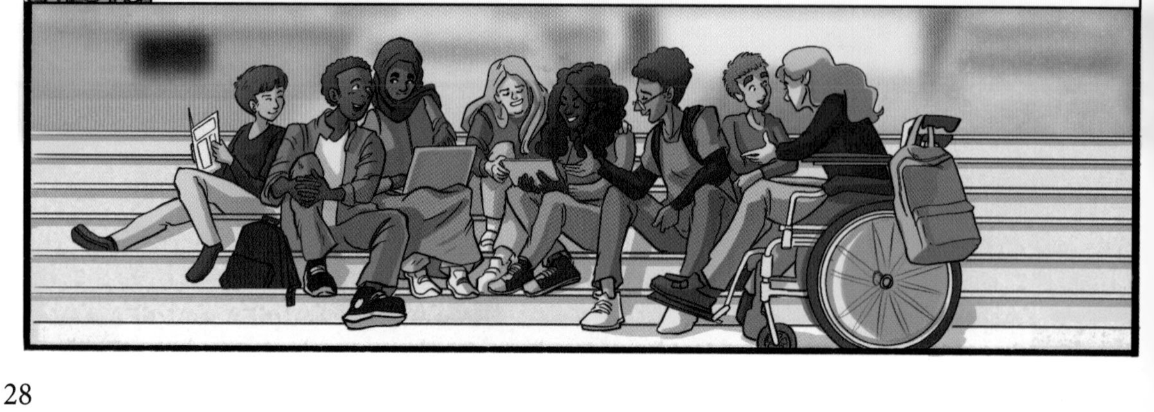

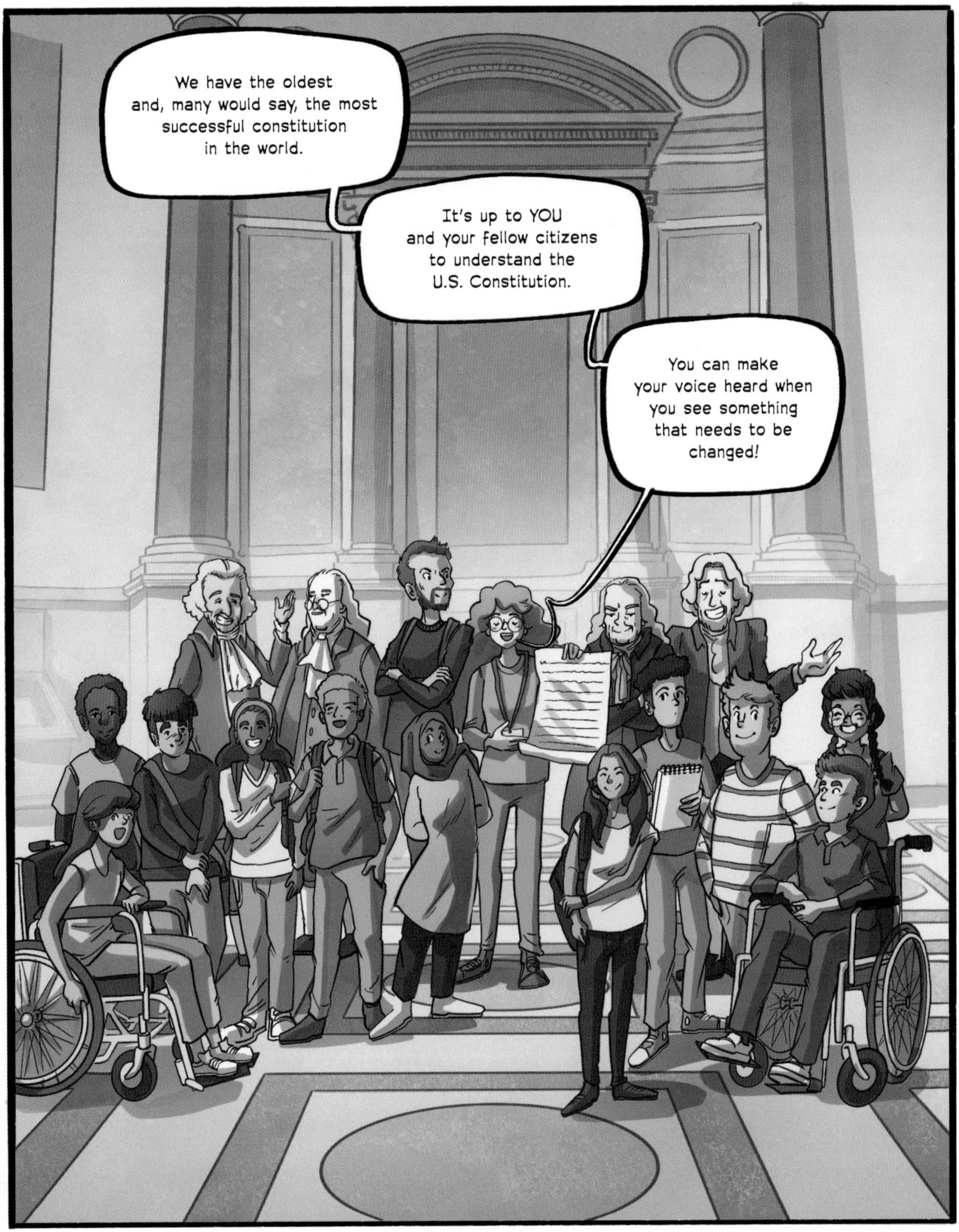
We have the oldest and, many would say, the most successful constitution in the world.
It's up to YOU and your fellow citizens to understand the U.S. Constitution.
You can make your voice heard when you see something that needs to be changed!

GLOSSARY

amendment (uh-MEND-muhnt)—a formal change made to a law or legal document, such as the U.S. Constitution

citizen (SI-tuh-zuhn)—a recognized legal member of a country

constitution (kahn-stuh-TOO-shuhn)—the basic principles and laws that determine the powers and duties of the government and guarantee certain rights its citizens

executive branch (ig-ZE-kyuh-tiv BRANCH)—the branch of government headed up by the president; it includes the president, the vice president, and 15 main executive departments

judicial branch (joo-DISH-uhl BRANCH)—the branch of government that includes the courts and judges; the highest court in the judicial branch is the Supreme Court

legislative branch (LEJ-iss-lay-tiv BRANCH)—the branch of government that creates the laws; it includes the Senate and the House of Representatives

ratify (RAT-uh-fy)—to formally approve

tax (TACKS)—money collected from a country's citizens to help pay for running the government

veto (VEE-toe)—the presidential power to reject a bill passed by Congress; if two-thirds of both houses pass the bill again, they override the veto, and the bill becomes law

READ MORE

Demuth, Patricia Brennan. *What is the Constitution?* New York: Penguin Workshop, 2018.

Kennedy, Katie. *The Constitution Decoded: A Guide to the Document That Shapes Our Nation.* New York: Workman Publishing Company, 2020.

Sheehan, Ben. *What Does the Constitution Say?: A Kid's Guide to How Out Democracy Works.* New York: Black Dog & Leventhal Publishers, 2021.

INTERNET SITES

Liberty's Kids: We the People
youtube.com/watch?v=ZJKaqn2RrQ4

National Archives: America's Founding Documents
archives.gov/founding-docs

National Constitution Center
constitutioncenter.org

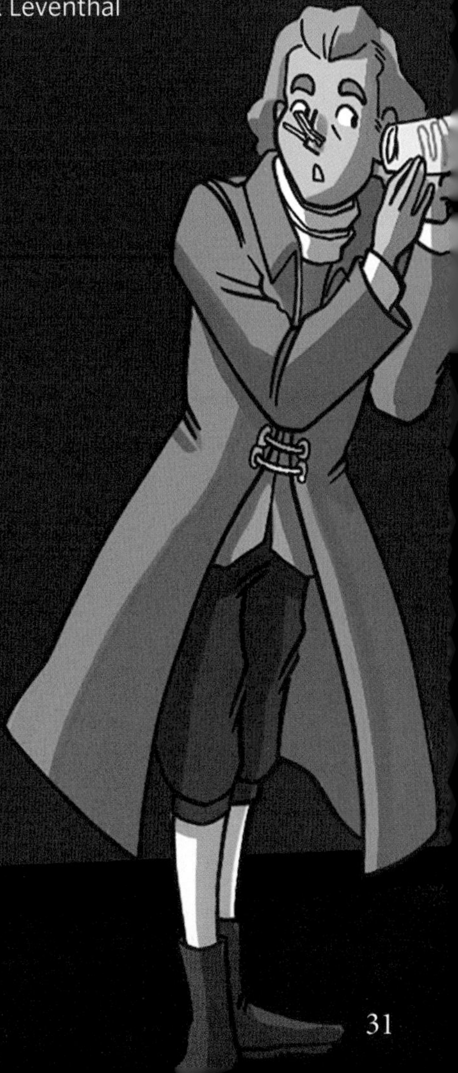

ABOUT THE AUTHOR

Sara Latta is the author of many books for children, middle grade, and young adult readers. She combines her academic background in science with a love for words to create nonfiction books and graphic novels that focus on science and nature, history, and biography. Her most recent biography, *I Could Not Do Otherwise: The Remarkable Life of Dr. Mary Edwards Walker*, won an Honorable Mention Grateful American Book Prize in 2023. She lives and works in New York City. Visit her online at www.saralatta.com.

ABOUT THE ILLUSTRATOR

Manu Molvar is a Sevillian illustrator based in Barcelona. He specialized in comics and albums for young people. Manu's style is influenced by the anime and cartoons he loved as a child, mixed with the baroque aesthetics of the traditions of southern Spain. With this medium, he uses a dynamic, colorful, and cheerful style so that no one suspects that, deep down, he is a drama queen.